RISE AND GROWTH OF CAPITALIST CLASS

RISE AND GROWTH OF CAPITALIST CLASS

(During Nineteenth Century)

V.S. MISHRA
Associate Professor, Deptt. of History
Vartak College of Arts,
Vasai Road (W) – 401 202, Distt. Thane

Commonwealth

Rise and Growth of Capitalist Class

First Published : 2011

ISBN 978-81-311-0378-4

Published by :
COMMONWEALTH PUBLISHERS PVT. LTD.
4831/24, Prahlad Street,
Ansari Road, Darya Ganj,
New Delhi - 110002
Ph. : 23272541, 23257835
Fax : 91- 011- 23257835
e-mail : commonwealthbooks@gmail.com

Laser Typesetting by :
Dimple Computers
Delhi

Printed at :
Roshan Offset Printers
Delhi

DEDICATION

To my father Shri Satyadev Prasad Mishra
(Symbol of Truth, Honesty and Integrety) and
to my mother Smt. Heera Devi Mishra
(Symbol of Priceless Values)...

FOREWORD

History deals with facts which are scientifically proved and are absolutely correct. Facts can be sifted, arranged and interpreted in such a systematic way that they must stand the test of time.

History is both a science and an art. Historian is like a craftman whose job is like a weaver who prepares warp of facts, uses his skills to weave by employing other facts as a waft. The end product naturally emerges as a piece that makes a convincing reading. This piece presents picture of a kaleidoscope but once rotated or shaken may present absolutely picture of another pattern.

The book 'Rise and Growth of Capitalist Class' (During Nineteenth Century) is a microscopic study undertaken by Dr. V.S. Mishra, Associate Professor Department of History at Vartak college, Vasai Road (W), Distt. Thane. He has exhaustively used various manuscripts lying in the files of General Administration, Finance, Judicial, Political, Revenue and Educational Department including letters from the East India Company. He has also used published works kept in the Archives Department of the government of Maharashtra.

The history of mankind during nineteenth century witnessed Industrial Revolution in Europe and it set the pace of progress in productivity on a fast track. It was a boon in one way but also a curse in its own way. It led to rise of Capitalism, Imperialism and Colonialism. Its full effect was seen in the twentieth century all over world. This led to the by product of Communism, an antithesis of capitalism. Communism brought about Russian Revolution – a great experiment in human history. Capitalism, of course, resulted into two World Wars and as time passed, Russian experiment failed leading to disintegration of U.S.S.R. Now that capitalism has led to globalization, it is important to probe deep into this system.

In this book, Dr. Mishra explores the conditions and circumstances that led to the rise of capitalist class in city of Bombay during 19th century. The contents of the book are divided into seven chapters.

In chapter I, titled *Introduction,* he traces the agrarian system of land tenure. To set the stage, he discusses Karl Marx's view on capitalism who describes it as a system in which a few individual possess capital for production and thereby make more money.

According to Dr. Mishra, capitalism leads to never ending process of profit making resulting into boundless greed. In pursuance of this passionate chase for profits, the British society underwent transformation from feudal system to capitalist system. In city of Bombay, various trading communities indulged in flourishing cotton and opium trade and became rich. The Parsis in particular made money through British connections. They acted as brokers to their establishment and thus earned huge profits.

In Chapter II, captioned as *Transformation of Land Relations (From Feudalism to Capitalism),* Dr. Mishra highlights how British capitalist class plundered and enslaved backward people in the continents of America, Asia and Africa. They used system of taxation, monopolies, system of protection (state support) for development of capital through the method of exploitation. These methods were also tried in India in general and also on the Island of Bombay.

East India Company continued feudal land relations in earlier days of its occupation of Bombay. In 1836, the Company made grants of Foras land in perpetuity. In 1851, the Foras Act of 1851 confirmed the holders of Foras land in their possessions. In 1822, Nawroji Jamshedji was put into possession of batty grounds in villages of Parel, Naigaon, Sion and Mahim by executing formal deed to gift enabling him to collect and raise revenue of gifted lands. Likewise a system of lease tenure of 21 to 999 years was also introduced in Mazgaon, Byculla, Colaba and Kamathipura.

Chapter III is titled *Mercantilism, Moneylending and Speculation (17th and 18th Century)*. Mercantilism denotes economic theory that helps generation of wealth and stimulated the accumulation by profitable balance which a government should encourage by means of protection. The chapter highlights how the Bombay merchants acted as junior partners of British merchants. Introduction of bills of exchange, Hundi system led to the rise of a separate class of moneylenders who granted loans on security of land, future harvest and stock of grains. The period also witnessed an emergence in speculative activities. Purchase and sale of produce still ungrown for future delivery was important. Expected produce was sold and resold over and over again. Marwaris, Banias of Gujarat actively participated in all such activities.

Chapter IV is captioned *Commercial, Trading and Money-lending Capitalists (1801-1850 A.D.)*. This chapter reveals how Bombay became main trade route of foreign trade which was also being extended into the interior. There was also an increase in overseas trade. The East India Company depended on resources of Gujarati, Parsis and Bohra merchants for export of opium. Bombay also emerged as a leading centre of shipbuilding. Industrial revolution in England enabled British industrial capital to turn whole of India into a market for their industrial products. According to Dr. Mishra, activities of big trade and moneylending firm best suited to the needs of British capitalist.

In chapter V, titled *Comprador Nature of Indian Industrial Capitalists (1851-1900 A.D.)*, Dr. Mishra highlights origin and growth of early entrepreneurship in India with special reference to Banias, Jews, Jains, Bhatias, Marwaris, Bohras, Khojas and Memons, etc. They all belonged to traditionally trading class and made full use of available economics opportunities. They acted as comprador capitalists and collaborated with the British in their economical activities by gaining commission. They also set up industrial enterprises and dealt with the European business houses. This led to establishing of cotton mills, textile industries, iron and metal mart. Besides, it also led to growth of economic nationalism and emergence of leaders like Dadabhai Nowroji, Phirozshah Mehta, M.G. Ranade and others.

Chapter VI is titled *Impact of Rising Capitalist Class (1801-1900 A.D.)*. During the 19th century, Indians received western education. English education proved useful and expedient and led to the creation of educated middle class. Christian missionaries continued to play their role in growth and development of educational institutions of Bombay. The new educated class of Indians supported liberalism, western ideological principles. The Indian National Congress became a rallying point for intellectuals who gradually began to demand share in the administration. It also created awareness amongst Indian intellectuals about ill-effects of British Rule.

The last and conclusive chapter deals with *Nature and Strength of Capitalist Class* at the end of the 19th century. Though the British capitalists in Bombay surpassed the Indian capitalists, the later became critical of former's preferential treatment together with undue restriction on Indian trade with non-British countries. Hence there appeared strong resistance to the British capitalists. Emerging intelligentia became responsible for showing to people of India, the real nature of British ruling class. It prepared background for freedom struggle not only in Bombay but whole of India.

The book indeed deals with a great theme of extraordinary history. It presents vivid and engaging reading. The contents of the Text make in depth study of a micro phenomenon with macroscopic significance.

Dr. V.S. Mishra has exhibited by writing this book a depth craftsmanship. He has prepared ground for further probe into the process of rise and growth of capitalism in India. By presenting this scholarly work, he has exposed the mystery that *in the drop is contained the ocean and the ocean is in the drop.* To unravel this mystery is by itself a big challenge that Dr. Mishra has posed before other historians.

Repetition of some facts in this work is only intended to lay more emphasis. I congratulate Dr. V.S. Mishra for this scholarly work. I am confident that publication of this book will prove as a first step on his long journey in the field of never ending historical research.

Mumbai 2010 **Dr. K. Jagjit Singh**

PREFACE

In the present study an attempt has been made to explore the conditions and the circumstances in which the Capitalist Class in Bombay (Mumbai) arose and grew up in the nineteenth century.

While selecting the theme for investigation, it was found that very few works have been done on the capitalist class and the majority of them are related to all India basis except V.I. Pavlov who has done some work on some of the capitalists of Bombay city. It was also found that the work on labour class and their movement in Bombay has also been done by many scholars but no one has ever tried in particular to study the origin and growth of the capitalist class in Bombay. Therefore, I decided to take up this theme.

While inquiring into the rise of capitalist class, I focused my attention firstly on tracing the population of the city of Bombay, first under the Portuguese occupation and later on under the British East India Company and then have gone to trace the agrarian system *i.e.* land tenure in the Island and City of Bombay which up till now remains untouched by the scholars. I have also described the contribution of various communities in general and the Parsis, Bhatias, Banias and Marwaris in particular. I have portrayed a picture of the contemporary social strata and their contribution to various enterprises such as ship-building, textile-mills, banking and money-lending, etc. with a view to analyses how the industrial class slowly emerged in the city of Bombay.

In the process of making investigation into the rise of capitalist class in the city and island of Bombay, the non-

Marxist approach of Dr. D.R. Gadgil is adopted who wrote "The Origin of Indian Business Class: An Interim Report." (Unpublished, New York,1959).

I also tried to discuss Max Weber's famous theory of the rise of industrial capitalist class from amongst communities in a country showing exception to his theory. I have analysed the rise of industrial class in Bombay from the communities such as Parsis as an exception to Max Weber's assertion on the emergence of capitalist class from amongst traditional business communities.

I have also traced the development of educational institutions which produced the class of professionals *i.e.* intelligentia. It contributed to the rise and growth of economic nationalism in the city of Bombay. It was this class that helped the Bombay capitalists to grow by collaborating with them in making the administration to work for their advantages by systematically waging intellectual war against the British rulers. No wonder the relationship between the Indian capitalists and the British administrators and industrialists changed from that of cordial friendship, to the 'competitive rivalry' with the passage of time. It was this class of intelligentia that indirectly helped the growth of capitalist class in Bombay.

The account given in this work is based upon the important primary sources obtained from the Archives of the State of Maharashtra and the secondary sources from the various libraries together with newspapers and journals of the time.

How far I have succeeded in my effort is left to the readers. But I hope that it would prove extremely useful to the students, teachers of the various universities where history of Bombay/ Mumbai is taught at various level. It would also be equally useful to the general readers as well. I'll be glad to have constructive suggestions and comments from the scholars and readers for my enlightment.

Mumbai-2010 **V. S. Mishra**

ACKNOWLEDGEMENTS

I have great many thanks to acknowledge for assistance in the writing of this book. My foremost debt is to my teacher Dr. R.R. Singh of G. N. Khalsa College, Matunga who always encouraged me to focus on my studies and gave suggestions to me even at the time when his health did not permit him to do so. He interacted with me more as a friend than a teacher without whom this work would have never been possible. I am also indebted to Dr. A. Cherian of Wilson College Chaupati, who too worked as an inspiratorial force to me in the completion of this work. In fact, both of them have provided stimulus and encouragement when it was much needed and have been forthcoming in their times when it was equally wanted.

My gratefulness is also due to the Director and the other staff of The Maharashtra Secretariat Record Office, Elphinston College Building, who not only allowed me to get access to the manuscripts and other published sources but also permitted me to take the Xerox copies of the records. I also record my thanks to the Librarian, Fort, as well as Kalina, Santacruz of University of Mumbai for their valuable assistance in locating the source material for my investigation. My thanks are also due to the Asiatic Society of Bombay Library and People's Free Reading Room and Library; Dhobitalao for their valuable help.

I must also record my sincere thanks to my colleagues and friends especially Prof. (Dr.) T.R. Ghoble, Deptt. of History, University of Mumbai and Dr. K.S. Cheema, former Chairman,

Board of Studies in History and Archaeology, **University of** Mumbai who personally helped me by giving **some materials** relevant to my study. I am also thankful to Dr. S.D. Pawar, former Prof. cum Director, Institute of Distance Education, University of Mumbai, Dr. V.K. Khade, (Principal of St. Joseph College of Arts and Commerce, Nalasopara, Distt. Thane and Dr. H.S. Gorge, Associate Professor & Head, Deptt. of History, R.K.Talreja College, Ulhasnagar,Thane who all not only encouraged me but also assisted in bringing this work to completion. There have been a large number of other individuals like *Prof. R.T. Sarode* and *Prof. A.B. Shirke*, my colleagues from Vartak College, Vasai Road who have been equally helpful and to these friends too, I offer my thanks.

I also offer my gratitude to my wife *Mrs. Pushpadevi Mishra* and my children *Miss Kanchan, Miss Upasana and Mr. Prashant Mishra* without whose help I would have never been in position to concentrate on my studies as they all kept me away from the household worries.

I shall be failing in my duties, if I do not express my thanks to Dr. K. Jagjit Singh, Former Professor, Guru Gobind Singh Endowment Chair, University of Mumbai, who agreed to write foreword of this book. While going through the text, he made several constructive and highly meaningful suggestions which enabled me to give a new outlook to the text.

Finally, I would also like to thank Commonwealth Publishers, New Delhi without whose help, this work would have never come into book form.

I am alone, of course, entirely responsible for the deficiencies of this work.

Mumbai – 2010 **V. S. Mishra**

Contents

1

Introduction

Karl Marx, one of the greatest interpreters and critics of capitalism defines capitalism as a system in which a few individuals possess capital for production and thereby make more money, transforming the previous equation of Commodity-Money-Commodity (CMC) into Money-Commodity-Money (MCM). According to V.I. Lenin, "Capitalism is the name given to that social system under which the land, factories, implements belong to a small number of landed proprietors and capitalists, while the mass of the people possess no property or very little property, and is capable of hiring out workers." Lenin points out two conditions for the emergence of capitalism, *first* that there should be enough people without either means of production or that of subsistence; hence they must sell their labour power, and *second* that there must be concentration of means of production and a large amount of money or funds in the hands of certain individuals. The American Dictionary of Philosophy defines 'Capitalism' as "A system of economic production which is characterized by the fact that the instruments of production (land, factories, raw-materials, etc.) are controlled to a greater or lesser extent by 'private individuals or groups'. Since an individual can exercise control over means of production, it is never absolute and as a matter of fact fluctuates widely with the ever-changing natural and social environment." [1]

Capitalism is a very loose term which covers a host of actually different economic systems. An application of this basic notion of individual control is that the individual will control production in his own interests. The ideological counterpart to this fact is the 'concept of profit' just as the ideological counterpart to the control itself is the myth of 'private property' and 'free enterprise'.[2] According to Karl Marx, in pre-capitalist system of barter, commodity transactions, commodity was exchanged for consumption which can well be explained in form of equation as Commodity-Money-Commodity, but in capitalist system transaction is always for money and more money, which can be explained as Money-Commodity-Money and more money. Then Marx says, "The circuit C-M-C starts with one commodity and finishes with another, which falls out of circulation and into consumption. Consumption, the satisfaction of wants, in one word, is value its ends and aim. The circuit M-C-M, on the contrary, commences with money and ends with money. Its leading motive and the goal is to attract, therefore mere 'exchange value".[3]

Karl Marx further says, "As the conscious representative of this movement, the possessor of money becomes a capitalist. It is person, rather his pocket is the point from which the money starts and to which it returns. The expansion of value, which is the objective basis or main spring of circulation M-C-M, becomes his subjective aim, and it is only in so far as the appropriation of ever more and more and more wealth in the abstract becomes, the sole motive of his operations, that he functions as a capitalist that is as a capitalist personified and endowed with consciousness and with use values must therefore never be looked upon as the real aim of the capitalist, neither the profit on any single transaction. Never ending process of profit making alone is what he aims at. This boundless greed after riches, this passionate chase after exchange value is common to the capitalist and miser. But while the miser is merely a capitalist gone mad, the capitalist is a rational miser. The never ending augmentation of exchange-value, which miser strives after, by seeking to save his money from circulation, is attained by the more acute capitalist, by constantly throwing it afresh into circulation".[4]

This is something which even Aristotle had observed in his remark that: "So far as it is the art of gaining livelihood, it is limited to procuring those articles that are necessary to existence, and useful to a household or the state. True wealth... consists of such values in use, for quantity of possession of this kind, capable of making life pleasant, is not unlimited. There is, however, a second mode of acquiring things, to which we may by preference and with correctness give the name of chromatistic, and in this case there appears to be no limits in riches and possessions. Trade.... Literally retail trade, and Aristotle takes this kind because in it values in use predominates, does not in its nature belong to chromatistic, for here the exchange has reference only to what is necessary to themselves (the buyers or sellers)..in the case of chromatistic circulation is the source of riches and it appears to revolve around money, for money is the beginning and end of this kind of exchange. Therefore of riches, such as chromatistic strives for are unlimited, just as every act that is not a means to an end, but an end in itself, has no limit to its aims because it seeks constantly to approach nearer and nearer to that end, while these acts that pursue means to an end, are not boundless, because the goal itself imposes a limit upon them. So with chromatistic, there are no bounds to its aims, these aims being absolute wealth. Economic not chromatistic has a limit... the object of the former is something different from money, since the time of Aristotle although they had not become the main part of trade as they came to be in the capitalist system. ..."[5]

This shows that the transactions for the sake of money were called on even at the first stage of the rise of capitalism that has been termed as '*Primitive Accumulation*'. '*Primitive Accumulation*', according to Karl Marx, "is nothing else than the historical process of divorcing the producer from the means of production".[6] The primitive accumulation. In Marx's analysis, took shape in its most typical from in England, where the landlords forcibly seized the common lands of the peasants and even evicted them from their homes. The landlords turned the land taken from the peasants into pastures for sheep or leased to farmers for the same purpose, their main aim being to increase the production of raw materials, wool, which was in great demand for the growing textile industry. The forcible expulsion of the peasants from land resulted in *(a)* land becoming the private property of a comparatively small group of individuals, and *(b)* guaranteeing of an abundant influx of wage – workers in to the industry. In his analysis of the process of accumulation of great wealth by particularly England for organizing its big capitalist enterprises. Karl Marx pointed out the following methods adopted by that country:

(i) The colonial system of plundering and enslavement of the backward people of America, Asia and Africa;

(ii) The system of taxation, creation of monopolies and the methods of appropriating major part of the taxes levied on population;

(iii) The system of protection-state support for the development of capitalist industry;

(iv) Brutal methods of exploitation. The methods, it is needless to assert, were employed by the British rulers in India, during the rule of the 'Raj" over India, with which every student of modern Indian history is amply acquainted. What is however needed is to study how was the process of exploiting of India for the development of British capitalism that inadvertently introduced some forms of capitalism in India.

As Indian society has been multi-sectoral it had to adjust to capitalist development in different way from the English society, hence there is need for sectoral study of capitalist development in India. The complexity of Indian problem in this regard has been described by D.R. Gadgil, an outstanding Indian economist in his very interesting and valuable '*Interim Report on the Origins of the Modern Indian Business Class,*' observes that "It became clear as one looked into the historical material through a number of monographs on particular periods or aspects that had appeared during recent decades, a comprehensive view of Modern Indian Economic History, especially, in relation to growth of modern business, had not been taken. The part of the task appeared, therefore, to be that of writing serious economic history even though based on secondary sources. As the field was almost unchartered, it became necessary to organize bit by bit the total data in some sort of meaningful sequence. The basic geographical characteristic of different regions, the changing political situation and politics of various regimes the qualities and the degree of adaptability displayed by particular business communities, the pervasive influence of British power and British business interests operating against the background of a technological and industrial revolution all these had to be taken into account for an understanding of the situation".[7]

In case of Marx and Engles, it can be said that they in their great work 'Capital' studied generally the British society which had undergone transformation from feudal system to capitalist system in almost purset form. They, therefore, gave the outlook and model principles, not laws and sub laws for the study of transformation from feudalism to capitalism of societies having complex forms unlike the purset form which the British society had, although they have given some idea about the study of such societies in their other works, particularly the *'Manifesto of the Communist Party'*.[8] V. I. Lenin clearly states that "Marx speaks of one formation of society only, the capitalist formation that is, he says that he investigated the law of the development of this formation only and no other".[9] Hence while inquiring into the transformation of Russian society from feudalism to capitalism in his work *'The Development of Capitalism in Russia'*, Lenin sets a model for studying the petty-commodity sector and various subsection of the capitalist sector in their interaction, without tackling every aspect of the general multi-sectoral problem. Later on Lenin studied Russian agrarian sector and interaction of capitalist sector with it, and ultimately he dealt with multi-sectoral form of Russian society in his writings about the New Economic Policy. All these indicate that though Marx and Engles analysis of purset form of transformation of the British society from feudalism to capitalism provided the social scientists with the phenomenon, Lenin's continuous study and analysis of transformation of a multi-sectoral society as that of Russia to capitalism supplied relevant principles for the study and understanding of such a phenomenon.

The Indian society has not only been multi-sectoral but complex historically because many developments in Indian society have occurred in different historical environments. V.I. Povlov very aptly remarks that "When we define the economy of rural elite strata in India in the 18th and 19th centuries as being feudal or the economy of urban handicraftsmen as being petty-commodity or petty-capitalist, we are merely carried to the point of research into this actual socio-economic content and internal economic relations. Indeed, the 'sector-wise' definition does not in itself allow us to draw a distinct line between the various types of relations of production. When for instance does the village commodity carpenter become a petty-commodity producer, and the well to do community member a small farmer or a feudal land-owner leasing out land? Similarly, if we start only from the quantity of the labour involved and its detailed division in the manufacture of sugarcane products in the Indian countryside, the establishment concerned would have to be classified as capitalist. But the data on the remuneration of the labourers and the element of the patronage in their relation with their employees suggest that such establishments were perhaps ancillary lines of production carried on by feudal type house holding proprietor among the rural elite'".

By contrast, in another socio-economic context an establishment based on the personal labour of the owner may be classified as capitalist. Thus, underdeveloped capitalist production, according to Lenin's definition, even simple commodity production becomes not only a reserve of capitalism but also one of its minor varieties. The category of the small scale bourgeoisie includes every small commodity producer who covers his expenditure by independent farming, provided the general system of the economy is based on capitalist contradictions. This kind of situation can hardly be discovered in India in the period under review, but what Lenin says provides yet another important methodological criterion for typisation.[10]

In the late-medieval period in India, sizeable relics of slaveholding and tribal relations continued to co-exist alongside the dominant feudal sector, and the element of the petty-commodity sector (including some pockets of capitalism), primarily in urban handicrafts, were also there. In fact, Indian feudalism was itself of multiple forms. All these produced an unused diversity in the conditions of the social being of the laboring masses of India and in the levels of their material and spiritual culture.

The long historical period in which laboring sections with different living conditions co-existed with each other may have endangered such a rigid religious fixation of it in the caste regulations of Hinduism, which however, allowed various interpretations, sectarian trends and philosophical lines. At any rate, there is need for a historical and sociological explanation of two clear cut distinctions between Hindus on the one hand, and Judaism, Christianity and Islam on the other. The open and direct establishment of social specifics in the values of social behaviours and vital claims, and tolerance of ideological pluralism among its adherents.

The socio-economic process which started in India after the British conquest, notably, the extension of the petty commodity on formation of capitalist sector, led to a further dichotomy of social being and consciousness. In the new conditions, labour and products of the labour, to use Marx's words, took shape, "in transactions of the society, of services in kind and payments in kind" (as under feudalism) but increasingly assumed "a fantastic form different from their reality."[11] Indeed, in his ordinary life the Indian cultivator or handicraftsman appropriated or, conversely, alienated his product not only through the mechanism of immediate and understandable personal relations but also through commodity exchange, where he was faced with "the whole mystery of commodities, all magic and necromancy that surround the products of labour as long as they take the form of commodities."[12] In this respect, the Indian laboring man is with a two-fold aspect: the personal in the much too familiar form of the tax collector who appropriated a part of his product, and in the mystical as the depersonified owner of the product produced by and unknown labourer in unknown conditions and an unknown costs.[13] Accordingly, the unpaid surplus labour here could be expressed either in the form of rent or of profit. That is why extra-economic coercive (taxes, rent and levies), trade and money lending, more or less purely capitalistic method of exploitation were applied to Indian working men. It is in this context that it can be taken as extraordinary step of the East India Company to turn land relations in the Island of Bombay as capitalist by a declaration in 1718[14] by ending feudal loyalties and making money payments such as rent taxes, etc. for land. The Company introduced farming of land and desolution of estates created by the Portuguese, Company's actions being the collection of money and money only.

The Parsis were the earliest immigrants to the Island of Bombay. Streynsham Master made, within three years from the date of cession of the Island of Bombay by Portuguese, a statement which runs as: "Here is also some Parsee, but they are lately come since the English held the Island and are most of them weavers and have not yet to do their devotion in or bury their dead."[15] The first Parsi to visit China was Hirji Jivaji Ready money in 1756 and he was followed by Jamshedji Jijibhoy, who made four voyages prior to 1807.

According to Gazetteer of Bombay City and Island, "In 1780, Parsis in Bombay numbered about 3,000, and this number was augmented by a great immigration from Gujarat in 1790, consequent upon a severe famine in that area. By 1811, the communities numbered more than 10,000, possessed landed property, and were partners in most of the big mercantile firms as well as shipbuilders and shipowners."[16] According to J. Forbes, "In the 70's and 80's of the 18th century, a considerable parts of land in Bombay belonged to Parsis, and also many beautiful houses which they had built themselves or bought from the Englishmen who had gone home."[17]

The Parsis made money through British connections as they acted as suppliers of necessary goods to the British troops in their war with Marathas, and also acted as brokers to the European mercantile firms, "After the European merchants came to India, brokerage became the main occupation of rich Parsis. Then the center of Parsi community was transferred to the English factory at Surat. When Surat's importance declined in the beginning of 18th century, the Parsis began to move to Bombay. According to tradition, first Parsi, Dorabji Nanabhoy had settled in Bombay as early as in 1640. Among those who took residence in Bombay in 1840's were Kuwarji Cama, the forefather of the well known magnets, Nushirvanji Wadia, the founder of the shipbuilding industry in Bombay, and Rustomji Dorabji whom the English later appointed Patel of Bombay."[18] Parsis were among early settlers in Bombay under the Company's control and as early as 1773, the Parsis from Gujarat, who were settled in Bombay, were allotted a separate district in the center of the town on Malabar hill.[19] In 1780, the population of Parsis in Bombay was 3,000, and a decade later, fleeing from starvation, many more Parsis moved from Gujarat to Bombay.

Writing about the Parsis, D. R. Gadgil says: "In Gujarat, apart from Hindu, Jain Banias and the Muslim trading communities, it is necessary to note the emergence of Parsis. This seems to have taken place chiefly in connection with the activities of the European traders at Surat and Bombay. From early times, Parsis established connections as brokers with European traders. A remarkable feature to be noted about is that their traditional occupations were not connected with trading or finance. In the accounts of 17th century travelers, they are noticed as artisans, carpenters, weavers, etc. Their prominence in Bombay was also established, in the first instance, through their shipbuilding activity. Though they later became dominant trading and financing community like other Gujarati, communities. Their original artisan background is an important feature that deserves notice."[20]

It is well known fact that at the beginning of the 18th century, the East India Company traded in Bombay through its official brokers. The brokers acted as commercial agents and also collected tax, when, however, the English established closer relations with local merchants, the privileged intermediary or broker became an impediment. In 1737, therefore, the system of brokerage was abolished. Justifying this decision, the Bombay Court declared: "We are satisfied our investment may be carried on behalf by contracting direct with the merchants, and that our duties of Consulate at Surat may be collected equally well by proper person appointed for the purpose. This we hope will also restore to 'our servants' trading from all parts of India to Surat, that perfect freedom of trade we would have taken enjoy, which they have made much continuous complaints they have hitherto 'not been able to obtain' being always obstructed by the power, interest, and influence of the broker."[21]

When the British used the methods of primitive accumulation to exploit India, Bombay traders were engaged in exporting goods, selling English manufactures in India and provisioning Bombay's population, garrison and fleet. In 1731, "Hindus, the Surat broker, having bought all the woolen goods, lead, copper and iron received by the ships last arrived from England, was as a sign of appreciation presented to the East India Company with a house worth Rs. 800."[22]

The Bombay traders had partnership with the British firms. According to one source (of 1828), every European trading establishment had a Parsi partner who usually provided most of the capital.[23] The colonial position of the country forced the Indian merchants to pay a kind of tribute to the powers represented by his British partner. Apart from Parsis, the Hindu trading communities Bhatia's and Banias (especially those of Kapol caste) arrived in Bombay somewhat later than Parsis. The Kapol Banias came from Gogha and Surat with their leader Shet Rupji Dhanji about the year 1756, while the Bhatia's came from Kathiawar and Cutch about the beginning of the nineteenth century.[24] "They voyage to Zanzibar, Muscat, China and Japan for trade purposes, but are forbidden by religion to journey to Europe and America."[25] Writing about Gujarat's Hindu trading communities, Christine Dobin Says: "There are two other leading Gujarati commercial communities in the city in the early nineteenth century. The Bania castes of Gujarat both Hindu and Jain had for long followed the occupation of brokers, traders and shopkeepers. From about 1670, there was a gradual immigration of Banias from Surat and other parts of Gujarat, where they too had assisted the Europeans in their commercial transactions to Bombay."[26] Because of their importance as bankers the Banias were active in the coasting trade between Bombay and the port of Kathiawar and the Konkan, from which they brought grains, vegetables, fruits, flowers and mutton for Bombay market. They also brought corn, cloth and later, cotton for export[27] of the Hindu Bania sub-castes in Bombay and by the middle of the century there were the Kopal Banias.[28] Kapol Bania families had been coming to Bombay since mid-eighteenth century although their leading family might have been in the city much earlier.[29]

Among the Jains, the outstanding community was that of the Dasa Oswal Banias. They had begun to leave Cutch for Bombay in the early nineteenth century.[30] Helping the East India Company to rob India, the Gujarati traders acquired considerable wealth. The English man John Burnell, who visited India in 1711, wrote "The Banias or merchants are not only rich and wealthy, but like the rest of the world are covetous after more, placing the height of their happiness in riches, which they will scrab together by mean and petty offices, some of them amassing prodigious sums of money, being accounted worth 90 or 100 lakh, or so many, times as 10,00,000.[31]

There were also three sects of Gujarati Muslim trading community in Bombay, *viz.*, Bohra, Khoja and Memon. The Boharas were descendants of converts from Hinduism to Islam in the eleventh century, who owed their conversion to Shia Ismaili missionaries sent to Western India by the Fatimid Caliphs of Egypt.[32] They had continued the occupation with commerce which had distinguished them as a Hindu caste, and were important traders in the Surat and Broach districts.[33] They had been in Bombay since the eighteenth century and were generally small businessmen trading with Gujarat and the

Northern India.[34] Parsis, Banias and Bohras dominated the trade of Bombay city in the eighteenth century and at the start of the nineteenth century. The two other rising communities, the Khojas and the Memons, were like Bohras, Hindu converts.

It seems probable that the Khojas represented a Bhatia sub-caste, while the Memons were converts from the Lohana and Cutch Bania castes. By 1840's so many Khojas had migrated from Cutch and Kathiawar that Bombay had become their head quarter, though at that time they had not risen higher than the status of small traders and were mainly seekers of parched rice. On the other hands, the Memons had a long history of contest with the European settlements though when they came to Bombay after 1813s famine in Gujarat, they started with tailoring and selling of fruits, and carried on furniture work and timber dealing.[35]

Muslim merchants in Gujarat, who had been trading long time since with the Middle East, were in the beginning political and commercial opponents of the East Indian Company. They were therefore at first unable to benefit fully from the developing trade. But from the beginning of the 18th century, the ties between the Muslim merchants and the English grew stronger. Their commercial activity in the service of the foreigners compensated the Muslim traders for the loss of so profitable a customer as the big Musalman feudal lords. The links between the East India Company and the Muslim merchant were, however, never as close as those with the Parsis or Hindus. The Muslims continued to trade along the old, established lines with the Middle East and Africa. Two Gujarati castes, the Bohras and Khojas, occupied a dominant position among the Muslim merchants.[36]

The Gujarati traders, Parsis and Hindus, made huge amount of money through cotton and opium trade. "Gujarat merchants also made vast fortunes on the opium trade and were beginning to export. In 1820's Gujarat compradors led by the prominent merchant Jeejijiboy started with the backing of the Maratha traders, to export cotton from Maharashtra.[37] Cotton export from Surat and Broach began even earlier and was still being carried on mainly by Indian merchants."[38]

The East India Company's interest in the collaboration of the Gujarati merchants forced it even in the 19th century to allow them to join in the trade with China, on 'excessive monopoly' which the company had jealously guarded against non-British European countries.[39] Opium cultivation in India was then concentrated in Banaras and Patna areas, and in the Malwa region, from where it was transported via Bombay to Canton. But the merchants of Eastern India were unable to derive great benefit from the trade in opium cultivated around Banaras and Patna, which the Company completely monopolized from 1799 to 1803. However, the merchants of Bombay sold opium and cotton to China, and imported tea and other goods, which were largely exported to Europe.[40] The British authorities controlled the opium trade in a dubious way. After the final conquest of the Maratha territories, the cultivation was made the exclusive privilege of Rajas of Indore, Gwalior and other local rulers. But the buying up of opium was the monopoly of the East India Company, which brought opium to Bombay and sold it by auction to local merchants. In 1831 the British scrapped their agreement with the Rajas and abolished the monopoly which Malwa had in the production of opium, while handling over the supplying of opium to private traders.[41] Large transit duties were levied on the opium being exported via Bombay harbour. A pound of opium sold in Calcutta in the mid 19th century brought the East India Company 7560 rupees of income, while the transit duties on opium going from Malwa gave the Company 55.8 per pound. The trade in Malwa opium was carried on directly by the Gujarat merchants. One of them, Hathi Singh who was the descendant of the Nagar Seths, a noted family from Ahmadabad, regularly sent large consignments of opium, containing upto 2,000 chests to China.[42]

In the first three decades of the 19th century, the Parsi Jamshedji Jeejeebhoy, one of the Bombay's richest merchants, made a profit of 30 million rupees on the opium trade, and deposited these to an English bank in Bombay.[43] Jamshetji Jeejeebhoy, in Miss Postan's estimate, in 1838 was the wealthiest Parsi merchant in Bombay who was born in 1783 in a Parsi family of meager means. He made his mark later in opium trade.[44] He managed to go to China where he traded in cotton and was unsuccessful and returned more poor, but the failure did not discourage him. He made three more journeys to China and made a fortune. Even the French navy, which operated along the shipping coast and once seized a vessel with a cargo belonging to him, did not stop him. He was connected with one of the leading firms in Bombay, Crawford and Co. In 1824, he headed a group of merchants who began to export cotton from Berar. Lastly, he had invested in the shipbuilding industry and was the biggest dock-owner, employing an average about 3000 hands.[45] Not only Jamshetji Jeejeebhoy but many other merchants of Gujarat, the grandfather of the mill-owners of Bombay and Ahmadabad made their fortune by trading in opium.[46] This trade in opium and other goods with China led to the rise of Bombay's shipping in the first half of the 19th century. The official list of 49 ships with a total displacement of 27,274 tons registered at the port of Bombay as of 1838, includes two ships (total displacement 2,002 tones) belonging to British companies. Twenty-two, and the biggest ones of that, were owned by Parsis. The other ship-owners were Muslims and Hindus.[47]

Companies registered in 1805

Firms owned by	*No. of firms*
Europeans	09
Parsis	16
Parsis-Chinese	02
Hindu	15
Muslims	04
Portuguese	03
American	04
Total	53

The following table reveals the national and religious, communal composition of the big merchants houses in Bombay at the beginning of the nineteenth century.

The above table indicates that nine leading private European firms were registered in Bombay in 1805, 16 Parsi firms and 2 Parsi-Chinese agencies, 15 Hindu firms, 4 Muslims, (Bohras), 3 Portuguese and 4 American firms.

Thus, 37 of the 53 Bombay firms belonged to Indians. But in spite of the numerical predominance of Indian firms, their commercial transactions were controlled by British merchant capital, which relied on the political power and the greater concentration of its capital.[48] Under such circumstances Indian capitalists became comprador capitalists. Writing about the development of Indian capitalist class from brokers to capitalists D. R. Gadgil says, "There are frequent references in the Surat records to the Company's brokers but it does not appear that this was necessarily a fix or permanently closed body or groups. The Europeans at Surat had dealings directly with large merchants and for financial accommodation they had to resort to the large Indian banking houses. The pattern evolved at Surat was appropriate to the condition of Europeans operating under the protection of Indian princes in large trading centers which had substantial Indian trading community."

This position appears to have changed with the formation of their own settlement by Europeans, especially when during the course of years Indian traders found it profitable to settle in the English settlements and began to be treated as subjects of the British Kings. In these settlements (such as Madras, Calcutta and Bombay) the Company dealt with merchants under them. The mode of transactions appears to be not brokerage but fixed contracts for transactions completed over a period.[49]

REFERENCES

1. V.I. Lenin : Collected Works, Vol. IV, p. 311.
2. Dagobert D. Runer (ed.) : *'The Dictionary of Philosophy'* (Philosophical Library, New York) 1942, p. 44.
3. Karl Marx and Fredrick Engels : *"Capital"*, Vol. I, p. 148.
4. *Ibid*, p. 151.
5. Aristotle: *'De Rep'* ed. : Bekkar, Lib-I-C-8-9, Quoted by Karl Marx and F. Engles: *Ibid.*, Vol. I, pp. 150-151.
6. *Ibid*, p. 714.
7. D.R. Gadgil: *"Origins of the Modern Indian Business Class—An Interim Report"* (New York, 1959) p. 111.
8. Karl Marx and Frederick Engles: *'Manifesto of Communist Party'* in Karl Marx and F. Engles *'Selected Works'* (2 Vols.) Vol. I (Moscow,1958).
9. V.I. Lenin: *'Collected Works'*, Vol. I (Moscow, 1963), p. 136.
10. V.I. Pavlov : *'Historical Premises for India's Transition to Capitalism'* (Moscow, 1979), pp. 9-10.
11. Karl Marx, *Op.cit.*, Vol. I, p. 77
12. *Ibid.*, p. 76.
13. V.I. Pavlov: *Op. cit.*, p. 19.
14. *"Gazetteer of Bombay City and Island"*, (hereafter to be referred as G.B.C.I.) Vol. II, p. 32.
15. *G.B.C.I.*, Vol. I, p. 194.
16. *Ibid.*
17. V.I. Pavlov: *"The Indian Capitalist Class: A Historical Study"* (New Delhi, 1964), J. Forbes: "Oriental Memoires," Vol. II, pp. 384-5.
18. V.I. Pavlov: *Op.cit.*, p. 90, *G.B.C.I.* Vol. I, pp. 132, 154.
19. C. Fawcett: *"English Factories in India"* (Oxford, 1936) Vol. I, p. 79.
20. D.R. Gadgil : *Op.cit.*, p. 20.
21. V.I. Pavlov: *Op.cit.*, pp. 91-92.
22. *Handbook for India* (Bombay, 1859) No. 30, Part-I, p. 263.

23. W. Hamilton: *East India Gazetteer* (London,1828), Vol. I, p. 261.
24. G.B.C.I., Vol. I, p. 168.
25. *Ibid.*
26. J. Douglas: *A Book of Bombay* (Bombay, 1883), pp. 85, 190.
27. G.B.C.I., Vol., I p. 410. M. Graham : *Journal of a Residence in India* (Edinburg, 1812), pp. 12,13.
28. *Times of India*, 13th February 1880, *Testimony of Witness in Kapol Bania Cooking Pats Case*, 23rd September 1879.
29. *Ibid.*
30. G.B.C.I., Vol. I, p. 168.
31. J. Burnell: *Bombay in the Days of Queen Anne* (London,1933), p. 110.
32. *Census of the City and Island of Bombay*,17th February, 1881, p. 46.
33. G. Briggs: *The Cities of Gujarashtra* (Bombay, 1840), p. 145.
34. William Milburn: *Oriental Commerce* (London, 1813), Vol. I, p. 171.
35. G.B.C.I., Vol. I, pp. 160,178. S.M. Edwardes: *The Rise of Bombay*, p. 236.
36. V.I. Pavlov: *Op. cit.*, p. 90.
37. *According to Dr.P.V. Kane & Dr. V.V. Mirashi, the origin of the term, 'Maharashtra' can be traced to the period of Satvahanas (about 200 B.C.) It should not be confused with the birth of linguistic State on 1st May 1960, as it represents territory inhabited by Marathi speaking people.*
38. V.I. Pavlov: *Historical Premises for India's Transition to Capitalism*, p. 326.
39. Karl Marx & F. Engles: Capital, Vol. I, p. 752.
40. V.I. Pavlov: *Op.cit.*, p. 328.
41. F.S. Turner: *British Opium Policy and its Results in India and China* (London, 1878)., pp. 55-56.
42. V. I. Pavlov: *Op.cit.*, p. 328, F.S.Turner: *British Opium Policy*, p. 56.
43. S.H. Jhabvala: Sir Jamshedji Jeejeebhoy, Baronet, (Bombay), p. 20.

44. V.I. Lenin: *Op. cit.*, p. 328.
45. Postans: *Western India in 1838,* Vol. I, p. 122.
46. V.I. Lenin: *Op.cit.*, p. 329.
47. *Ibid.*
48. V.I. Pavlov: *The Indian Capitalist Class*, p. 91.
49. D.R. Gadgil: *Op.cit.*, p. 42.

2

Transformation of Land Relations

(From Feudalism to Capitalism)

In his analysis of the process of accumulation of great wealth by particularly England for organizing its big capitalist enterprises, Marx pointed out four methods adopted by that country. Firstly, the colonial system: the plundering and enslavement of the backward people of America, Asia and Africa. Secondly, the system of taxation: creation of monopolies and the methods of appropriating major part of the taxes levied on population. Thirdly, the system of protection: state support for the development of capitalist industry and fourthly, brutal methods of exploitation. These methods were, it is needless to state, employed by the British rulers, and during the rule of the 'Raj' over India, with which every student of modern history is fully acquainted. What is, however, needed is the process of exploiting India for the development of British capitalism and the introduction of some forms of capitalism that was set in here. As Indian society has been multi-sectoral it happened to adjust to capitalistic development in different way from the English society, hence the need for sector-wise study of capitalistic development arises. Marx in his classic Capital studies only the British society which had undergone the transformation from feudal system to capitalist system in purest form. He, therefore, gave only the outlook and model principles, not laws and sub-laws for the study of the transformation from feudalism to capitalism of societies having complex forms unlike the purest form which the British society had. V. I. Lenin clearly states that "Marx speaks of one formation of society only that is capitalist formation, that is he says that he investigated the law of development of this formation only and of no other."[1] Hence while inquiring into the formation of Russian society from feudalism to capitalism, Lenin in his work *'The Development of Capitalism in Russia'* sets a model for studying the petty commodity sector and various such sections of the capitalist sector in their interaction without tackling every aspect of the general multi-sectoral problem[2]. Later on Lenin studied Russian agrarian sector and interaction of capitalist society with it, and ultimately he dealt with multi-sectoral form of Russian society in his writings about the New Economic Policy. All these show that though Marx's analysis of purest form of transformation of the British society from feudalism to capitalism provided the social scientists with the scientific outlooks and general model methods for the study of such phenomenon, Lenin's continuous study and analysis of transformation of a multi-sectoral society as that of Russia to capitalism supplied relevant principles for the study and understanding of such a phenomenon.

Indian society has been not only multi-sectoral but complex one historically because many developments in Indian society have occurred in different historical environments which produced multiple form of feudalism and created unique inter sectoral relations and complex interaction among them. This may be the reason why it is quite difficult and theoretically dangerous to envisage any conceptual criteria to fix common stages for transformation of Indian society from feudalism to capitalism. Perhaps V. I. Pavlov was faced with such a complexity of Indian situation in his study of India's transition to capitalism which made him to preface his study with an observation as follows:

> "Thus, when we define the economy of the rural elite's strata in India in 18th–19th centuries as being feudal or the commodity or petty capitalist, we are merely carried to the point of research into the actual socio-economic content

and internal economic relations. Indeed the 'sector-wise' definition doesn't in itself allow us to draw a distinct line between the various types of relations of production when, for instance, does the village community carpenter became a petty commodity producer, and well-to-do community member, a small farmer or feudal land owner leasing out land? Similarly, if we start only from the quantity of labour involved and its detailed division in the manufacture of sugarcane products in the Indian country side, the establishments concerned would have to be classified as capitalist. But the data on the remuneration of the laborers and the element of patronage in their relation with their employers suggest that such establishments were perhaps ancillary lines of production carried on by feudal type of house holding proprietors among the 'rural elite'."[3]

Such being the state of multi-sectoral Indian society it is safer to study a single development of the mechanism and the transformation to capitalism in the transformation of land relations in the City and Island of Bombay because Bombay is supposed to be one of the pockets of early capitalistic developments in modern India. A few scholars have carried out commendable studies on the beginning of capitalistic, commercial and industrial enterprises consequent upon the emergence of commercial and industrial capitalists in Bombay,[4] but no attempt has been made to inquire into transformation of feudal land relation to capitalist one. The attempt in this work therefore, is to trace out the stage of which a beginning was made to transform land relations to capitalistic land relations in the City and Island of Bombay.

At the outset of this inquiry, it is imperative to accept that few changes in land relations in the City and Island of Bombay at the early stage may not be sufficient pre-conditions for the transformation from the feudal stage to the capitalistic one because that involves a host of questions such as what was the state of production from land and whether that was confined to subsistence level or to some extent surplus? Who was the chief consumer of surplus product? What was the state and nature of feudal rent and which local feudal lord appropriated this rent? What was the state of and role of money during those days? What was relation between town of Bombay and countryside adjacent to it? What was the nature and volume of local, country and foreign trade at and through Bombay? What was the state of science and technology in Bombay and how much of them were applied to the agricultural production and so on?

Without going into the problems to seek the answers to the above mentioned questions this attempt is confined to the simple study of land relations in Bombay. This study is however, prompted owing to three reasons: *First,* most of the recent studies of Bombay narrate its history with reference to its commercial and industrial developments which have become almost repetitive exercise. *Second,* of late the increasing trend for the study of urban formation in Bombay or its urbanization is again repetitive with nothing new, except use of some fashionable terminologies, to the existing knowledge of the subject, and *third,* casual remark by the compiler of the Gazetteer of Bombay City and Island as follows:

"In 1718, a quit-rent was imposed to reimburse the Company for the charges they were put for fortification. This tax may be said to have substituted money for the liability to military service, and ended the feudal tenure."[5]

To begin with it is a statement of fact that the island of Bombay was given to the Portuguese by Sultan Bahadur Shah of Gujarat under a peculiar circumstance by the Treaty of Bassein signed on 23rd December 1534[6]. The surrender of Bassein and Bombay to the Portuguese was, however confirmed by the treaty of peace and commerce between the two on the 25th October 1535. After taking the possession of Bombay the Portuguese parceled out lands in the island of Bombay to the officers who had rendered single military service. These were known as Aforamento (hiring or renting) grants, which implied holding on a Fero or somewhat quit-rent varying from 4 to 10 percent of the usual rent.[7] Some of these grants for one or three lives, always with a renewable clause, and some vested in females and considered as their dower.

These gifts in absence of a female successor reverted to the state.

The above mentioned grants by the Portuguese government carried with them certain obligations of a feudal character as the grantees had to serve the king whenever occasion arose and attend on demand with a certain body of men fully equipped according to the rank. Subletting was permitted on practically the same terms. Besides, the Portuguese government received subsidies and free donations towards the public charge of the state.

In the beginning of the possession of Bombay, the Portuguese government created the Portuguese landlords by distributing estates as follows: Bombay proper was left to one Mestre Diogo, as tenant or foreito, for an annual quit-rent of about Rs. 537-3-0 payable at the royal treasury in Bassein.[8] The Island or Kasba of Mahim was similarly rented for about Rs. 751-1-3-0 and the Mandovin, i.e. the Mandvi or custom house of Mahim for about Rs. 178. Between 1545 and 1548, during the viceroyalty of D. Joao de Castro, the four villages of Parel, Vadala, Sion and Varli were granted to manual service for an annual payment of Rs. 158-8-0, the village of Trombay, Chembur to Dom Roque Terrode Menenszes, Elephanta Island to Joao Pirez for about Rs. 39-6-0 and the revenue of the custom-house at Walkeshwar to one 'Posagy' for Rs. 1-4-0.

It cannot be definitely stated for how long Mestre Diogo enjoyed the manorial right of Bombay proper, but it appears from different accounts that about the year 1554 during the viceroyalty of Dom Pedro Mascarenhas, the island was granted to Garcia da Orta, the celebrated physician and botanist, for a yearly rent of about £ 85 sterling.[9] Bombay apparently remained in his possession until his death in Goa in 1570 after which it appears to have been granted on the same tenure to several parties in succession, the last of whom was Donna Ignez Miranda, widow of Don Rodrigo Moncanto.

The Portuguese rule of Indian territories was not only feudal but theocratic, the keynote of their policy being embodied in Vasco-da-Gama's famous remark; Vimos *buscar christoas-e-speciana'* (we come to seek Christians & spices) and on this it is aptly remarked "the Christian was in their eyes of more importance than the spices."[10] Having converted about ten thousand natives in Başsein, Thane, Mandpeshwar and neighbouring places the Franciscans set to not only convert native population in bombay but to gain the over lordship of bombay in defiance to that of king of Portugal.

It was with the opening of the Portuguese rule that one Francis Antonio de Porto, a Franciscan friar, set sail for Bassein and Bombay. The Franciscan Mission was followed in 1542 by a Jesuit Mission. Both the missions vied with one another in the erection of churches and conversion of the inhabitants in bombay.[11] By 1585, the Franciscans had secured practical control of Salsette, Mahim, Bombay and Karanja Islands. By the close of the sixteenth century with exception of areas like Bombay proper and Mazagaon, which were granted to distinguished individuals, the bulk of land in the island of Bombay had fallen into hands of religious orders. The Jesuits appropriated largest share and were virtually, proprietors of all the northern areas of the island such as Mahim, Dadar, Matunga Sion, Sevri and Parel. They destroyed Hindu temples and Muhammadan mosques and carried out forced conversion, which led to the flight from Bombay of a large number of those people who did not succumb to the pressure to convert to Christianity.[12]

Surprisingly, these Roman Çatholic ecclesiastics earned larger revenue than even the King of Portugal himself. They defied not only the administrative representative of the king of Portugal but went to the extent of denying that the king was the lord of their possessions in India so much so that the Archbishop of Goa was compelled to complain to the king of Portugal against the Jesuits in 1629 and the Viceroy of Goa was compelled to tell the king in 1681 that the Jesuit priests and monks paid no heed to his orders. They retained armed bands at their own expense and actually waged war by sea against His Majesty's captains.

The Roman Catholic ecclesiastics lived sumptuously and

wielded a lot of influence in Bombay. One of the richest churches in Bombay was the Dadar Church which possessed landed property, cocoa-nut oarts, three affiliated chapels at Parel, Varli and Matunga, and a large house. In the same way the church property—The land, cocoa-nut oarts, large houses, etc., existed in many areas. The priests in these churches had insatiable avarice to acquire valuable land and plantation. These facts obtruded themselves upon the Reverend John Ovington, who visited Bombay in 1680 and remarked that "Few men can enjoy very peaceful lives who have any fair possessions near the convents of the Jesuits, a pleasant seat and a fruitful plantation can hardly escape their gaining."[13]

In early years of the Portuguese take over, the population of the City and Island of Bombay was quite large considering the conditions of those days but it slowly got thinned due to forcible conversion by the Portuguese and that too during later part of the Portuguese rule over the Island of Bombay. An account of 1634 indicates that Bombay proper contained "eleven Portuguese families or married men (Cazados), and some native blacks (Pretes naturaes), making altogether, seventy musketeers able to serve in the war." The Kolis formed the major portion of the population, dwelling in most part of the island from Kolaba in the south to Sion and Mahim in the north. Then there were Kunbis and Agris, who cultivated the fields and served them with rice and all sorts of pulses. There were Malis, who tended the orchards, there were Bhandaris known as the men-at-arms. In Mahim, Bombay and Parel lived Prabhus "who collect the rents of the kings and of the inhabitants and their estates, and are also merchants." From Dhobi Talao to the Fort of Malabar Hill were orchards and groves and several houses of the Indo-Portuguese, Bhandaris, Kolis and Agris were scattered among those groves. "North of Dongri, inhabited by Kolis and perhaps by a few Prabhus and Brahman inhabitants, lay the island and manor of Mazagaon, which served as the home of Portuguese, Kolis, Malis, Bhandaris, and perhaps a few Hindu Serivains (clerks). In northern islands were Jesuits, who owned houses, and demesnes in Parel, Sion and Mahim. The later island was probably inhabited by small numbers of the Portuguese, by Prabhus, Brahmans of Palsikars or Shenvi caste, a few Muhammadans and the lower classes of Hindus. Similarly at Naigaon the Prabhus and Brahmans must still have been resident, though the latter found it harder than the former to maintain a livelihood and reputation amongst those who had been largely persuaded or forcibly driven to become Christians. The Prabhus, on the contrary became men of business, could still comfortably subsist by petty trading or by acting as rent-collectors and agents of Portuguese landlords."[14]

The chief product of the island during the Portuguese period were the cocoa-nuts, palm, brab, jack tree, jambul, the jangoma, and mango trees. Although some pulses were produced on the island cocoa-nuts and rice were stable products of the major part of the island, more so of the island of Mahim, Mazagaon and Sion noted for their saltpans, while the numerous settlements of Kolis were responsible for a large supply of fish, which was dried upon the island for sale to Moors. Although there is no proper account of the product of island of Bombay during the period of Portuguese rule, the end of that period and on the occasion of the possession of the Island by the English, and account of the produce of all lands of island was taken which showed the annual produce worth 80,000 xeraphins or Rs. 43,636/- and the actual income worth 20,000 xeraphins. As the population of the island then by all account was above 10,000 [15] the value of produce in no way shows that the people in general produced above subsistence level. All narration of the period indicates general poverty of the people, generally of the natives. The income of the island also indicated no lucrative gains to the Portuguese landlords and the king of Portugal. Hence, at no level the question of surplus arises. Even if there was some gains to the Portuguese landlords and the king of Portugal, those went to their personal accounts for their luxurious living rather than for production of any further capital or reproduction. The reason for this state of affairs was the feudal nature of Portuguese imperialism. All these indicate that the land relations in the Island of Bombay remained feudal in nature under the Portuguese rule. Actually speaking after the possession of the island of Bombay, there continued the existing medieval system of administration of land, preserving almost traditional land relations. It is therefore correctly observed that "of the system of administration during the epoch of Hindu and Musalman sovereignty no record remains, save the remark of a few Portuguese writers to the effect that the land was rented annually for a fixed sum of money during the period of Muhammadans rule, and that this system may have been in vogue at the time of Raja Bimb."[16] It is clear, however, that when the Portuguese obtained the possession of the Island, they found a land system resembling that which had been obtained in Goa since its conquest in 1510, and on that account introduced little or no alteration in it.[17] There increasingly developed during the Portuguese rule feudal tenure of feudal tenancy which is expressed by two Portuguese word in vogue... first was known as Aforemento which involved both a right and a duty, "the right to enjoy and the duty to defend the land, and was styled Aforemento or holding on payment of a foro quit-rent varying from 4 to 10 percent, of the usual rental."[18] Subletting was permitted on practically the same terms. Second, there also existed a minor tenure known as Arrendamento signifying the annual renting of land for a fixed sum in cash or kind. There also existed a tenure known as 'Pension' or 'Pencoa tenure'. The term 'Pension' takes its origin from the Portuguese word 'Pencoa' which means, when applied to the estate, a payment for enjoyment of land, the bonus or the premium paid for the fee-simple on the compromise of doubtful tenure. "This tenure appears to have been prevailing since the days of the Portuguese occupation of Bombay. Under this tenure no rates and assessment were fixed and it was not a quit-rent. It was only a royalty rent acknowledging the king of Portugal as lord paramount."[19] There was another tenure known as Forastoka, which also originated during the administration of the Portuguese government. With a view to encouraging industry and agriculture that government allotted to the cultivators the Tokabatty ground, certain pieces of land of an inferior quality subject to the payment of a very small rent denominated as

'Foras". This species of land was therefore usually styled by the natives 'Tokache Foras' that is Foras grounds attached to Tokabatty grounds.[20]

The Foras tenure was identified as the land reclaimed from the sea, and was also known as 'salt batty' ground. It appears from the English words that this originated during the English period as it is maintained that the old batty grounds were recovered from the sea by means of the vellard between Sion and Mahim. There is, however, a mention that in the middle of the sixteenth century the Portuguese financier Simao Botelho advised the king of Portugal to substitute for the grant of villages to deserving individuals for the allotment in perpetuity of submerged lands, to those who drained and reclaimed them, [21] and there is no doubt to believe that some land might have been reclaimed during the Portuguese period, which might have originated Foras tenure during the Portuguese period though that might have been insignificant. Similarly, even the Fazindari sub-tenure appears to have originated during the Portuguese rule as under this tenure land was let for building purpose, might be a house or hutment dwelling, without any formal agreement, and subject to a low annual ground rent. As it was a sub-tenure between a private proprietor and his tenant, the Portuguese landlords or the Portuguese landowners might have introduced this tenure for making some gains from the native inhabitants, constructing their houses or tenements or even thatched hutments.

Bombay was to be handed over to the British as a sequel of marriage treaty between Charles II and Infanta Catherine of Portugal on the 23rd June 1661. The actual cessation, however did not take place until 1664 when Humphry Cooke, successor of Sir A. Shipman, was practically made to accede to a treaty with the Portuguese on the following conditions:

(i) That the Kunbis, Bhandaris, and the rest of people bound to serve landowners or inhabitants of the villages under the Portuguese jurisdiction shall not be admitted at Bombay,

(ii) That every person possessing revenue of Bombay

either Patrimonial or Crown lands shall possess the same by right and shall not be deprived thereof except in cases which the law of Portugal directs,

(iii) That the inhabitants of Bombay and the landowners of that island shall not be obliged to pay more than the Foras they used to pay to Portugal, and

(iv) The Portuguese residents shall be exempted from the payment of customs and shall have liberty of trade from Bandra and the creeks of Salsette.

The above mentioned conditions indicate that the Portuguese wanted the British to continue their feudal practices in Bombay. The King of England disapproved these conditions and appointed Sir Gervase Lucas to supersede Humphry Cooke as the Governor of Bombay. Sir Gervase Lucas arrived in Bombay on the 5th November 1666. He found that Cooke while increasing the income of the king of England pocketed a sum of 12,000 xeraphins extorted from the inhabitants. Sir Lucas raised King's income from Bombay and died in Bombay on 21st May 1667. He was followed by Captain Garry as the Governor of Bombay. He also raised the income of the king of England from Bombay but during his tenure of office the Crown decided to handover Bombay to the East India Company, which took place by letters patent dated the 27th March 1668. During the rule of the Crown between 1664 and 1668 the income from Bombay was raised to 25,920 xeraphins though this collection was carried out by inquiry into the titles of land-holders and seizure of lands and estates of several people.[22]

The East India Company was granted the port and island of Bombay on an annual rent of $ 10 and the Company's representative, Sir George Oxinden, the President of Surat Council took the possession of it in the name of the Company on the 21st September 1668. By that time England, the homeland of the East India Company, had gone through transformation of its society from feudalism to capitalism as Karl Marx puts, "The prelude of the revolution[23] that laid the foundation of the capitalist mode of production, was played in the last third of the 15th and the first decade of the 16th century."[24]

Although in nature capitalist; the East India Company after taking the possession of Bombay first of all continued the Portuguese period's feudal land relation with tendency towards capitalist one and made capitalist within half-a-century of its rule. It can, however be said that after having secured the possessions of Bombay, the East India Company started semi-feudal and semi-capitalist land relation as it confirmed the Portuguese land tenure but raised the income from land in Bombay, and slowly introduced new land relation for capitalistic exploitation of the land and inhabitants particularly tenants of Bombay. This can be verified from the perusal of what the Company did since its possession of Bombay. The Company at the onset realized that during 1664-8 when Bombay was under the Crown the inquiry into the titles and assessment of land-holders had caused enough injustice and discontent. It therefore, instructed its President, Mr. Gerald Aungier "to forgo inquiring titles, and in conjunction with the landholders to fix a lump-sum as their rent payment, leaving their senior landholders to all of his share to each individual holder." This led Mr. Aungier to summoning a General Assembly of the chief representatives of the people of Bombay to be held at the castle of Bombay on 1st of October 1672.[25] Whatever were discussed in the Assembly were to be concretized by the representatives of the people as their proposal and be finalized and confirmed as agreement in another assembly to be held shortly. Thereupon the representatives of the people on 4th October 1672, presented a paper of their proposal containing twelve articles for another debate and consideration in the next assembly. That assembly was held in Bombay Castle on 1st of November 1672 in which the forms of twelve articles of the proposal were seriously discussed and finalized it into 14 articles as follows:

(*i*) That in consideration of the 20,000 xeraphins to be paid annually as three payments into the Honourable Company's treasury, the said Governor and Council do on behalf of the Honourable East India Company promise to put a final end to all claims, pretences, and law suits whatsoever which have arisen or may arise between the Honourable Company and the people touching the titles, lands or estates of palmgras cocoa-nut trees or batty grounds throughout the whole isles excepting what is by joint agreement excepted.

(ii) That the present possessors be granted new patents confirmed according to the respective titles, by which their heirs and successors shall enjoy their estates.

(iii) That if the Governor and his Council at present in power, or their successors shall think good, on behalf of the Honourable Company, to exempt any person enjoying the said land from paying his proportion of the said contribution, or shall make use of any part of the said lands for the necessary occupation of the public abatement shall be made out of the said contribution, in proportion to the lands so exempted or disposed of, and this in respect of the said contribution made upon all the estates and lands inheritance or the whole isle.

(iv) That all the estates of the batty grounds and cocoa-nut trees seized by former governors and now in possession of the Honourable Company shall be restored to their respective owners, and they, their heirs and successors confirmed in their said possessions as above is expressed.

(v) That if, in time to come, any of the said lands or estates shall fall to the Honourable Company for any title whatsoever, as also if any tree shall be cut down, or any oarts of batty ground made use of for the building of cities, towns or fortifications, then the value of the said lands or trees shall be computed, and a proportionable abatement made out of the contribution as is expressed in the third article.

(vi) That as the particular of dunging the palmgras and batty grounds with fish it is agreed upon by the Governor and Council and grant of as much import to the contribution that what part of the isle has this year been permitted to be dunged with babaxim shall be still permitted reserving the ground which is comprehended within the line of the city which by god's assistance is intended to be built. But in respect of the above said dunging the ground is forbidden generally by express orders from the Honourable Company of London it is necessary that their license be had thereunto. For the effectual securing of this it is convenient that the people do send their humble petition to the Honourable Company by their ships, and the Governor and Council will intercede on their behalf and doubt not but they will be pleased to confirm the grant, seeing that it is profitable to the public.

(vii) That in case hereafter by any storm or calamintors accidents (which God diverts), part of the said lands or estates be destroyed or rendered incapable of bearing fruit. It shall be referred to Governor and the Council to make such reasonable allowances or the contribution, as shall consist, with good conscience, and case of the inhabitants

(viii) That for the greater convenience and ease of the people in raising the said sum of 20,000 xeraphins per annum liberty shall be granted to the interested to nominate and appoint from among themselves such persons of sober and honest reputation as they shall think fit for the proportionable evaluation of all estates and lands and for the collecting and receiving of the said money and paying it, into the Honourable Company's treasury, which said person to be confirmed by the Governor, and shall take an oath on the holy evangelists to deal fastly and impartially with all. That the Honourable Company shall not be at any charge in receiving the said sum. But for the greater authority and accommodation of the said persons so appointed, two officers shall be ordered by the Governor on behalf

of the Honourable Company to assist them in their said office, as occasion shall require.

(ix) That all royalties, rights, privileges, and immunities which did formerly belong to the Crown of Portugal of Foras and Royal rents of what nature or condition whatsoever shall be reserved as of right they belong to the Honourable Company.

(x) That in regard the little isle Calio (Colaba) reaching from the outer point westward of the isle Paccart (Pakhadi or Parish) called Polo (Palav-Apollo) will be of great use to the Honourable Company, in the good design which they have for the security and defense of this whole isle, it is hereby agreed that it shall be totally and wholly reserved for the use of the said Company they making such reasonable satisfaction to the persons interested therein as hereafter is expressed.

(xi) That whereas by the manifesto presented by the people the first payment of the 20,000 xeraphins should begin on the 9th of February next ensuing, it is agreed that the first payment due on the 9th February shall be suspended to the 9th June following the year 1673 in which said sum shall be left in the hands of the people, by the Governor and the Council, towards purchasing and buying out those persons who have estates and lands in the Calio, whom they are obliged to satisfy in their respective demands, provided that the people shall pay the quit-rent due on the 9th February as was formerly accepted.

(xii) That in regard the Company, have expressly ordered a survey to be taken of the whole isle, it is necessary that the lands and estates of each person be measured, the charges whereof shall be limited with a fast moderation for the ease of the people.

(xiii) That there shall be reserved for the Honourable Company all grounds on the water-side within the compass of the isle to be disposed of on necessary occasions for the public excepting such grounds

wherein there are at present planted gardens of cocoa-nut trees or rice grounds, as also churches, houses or warehouses of stone. And whatsoever, for the public good it shall be necessary to make use of any of the said places or properties of the Governor and the Council shall make satisfaction to the interested in a reasonable manner. But the people are to take notice that in this they receive a particular favour from the Honourable Company, their Governor and Council, in regard that in all kingdoms of the world the ground on the waterside from the distance of 40 yards at least from high watermark belongs as a sovereign right and privilege to the King or Prince thereof.

(xiv) That seeing, the principal aim and intention of this happy agreement and composition is designed for the security, tranquility, peace and universal control of the respective inhabitants the Governor and Council do on behalf of the Honourable Company establish and ratify this agreement, as perpetual and irrevocable between the Honourable Company and the people and for the further satisfaction of the inhabitants and the people they do promise to prevail with the Honourable Company to establish and confirm the same by patent made under their hands and seals and given under one hand sealed in the Bombay Castle, the 12th November 1672.[26]

This agreement it is clearly maintained, remained a dead letter upto 1674 when President Aungier held his famous convention and drew upon an order, which though not ratified and signed by East India Company, seems to have been regarded as valid and was acted upon.[27] What is remarkable in this context is that the East India Company did not sign and ratify the agreement, leaving scope to dishonour the agreement as and when required.

This agreement though made the tenure of land under it as feudal but that was indeed, semi-feudal and semi capitalist as it recognized all land then occupied as private property subject to military service. The recognition of private property in land was a capitalist process while the condition of the military service was feudal. It is worth noting that the compiler of the Gazetteer of Bombay City and Island, while commenting on Mr. Arbuthnot's contention in 1876 with reference to Toka lands says, "Apparently, however, it was not the right of the Company as proprietor that was founded on the 9th article right to establish the system of taxation prevalent in the island under the Portuguese government. That article reserved the right of the Company to military service."[28] It is needless to state that the Honourable Company always regarded itself as the proprietors of land and as lords of the soil which were repeated in many of the orders of the Company.

Unlike the Portuguese king the East India Company was a capitalist enterprise, it was, therefore, interested in raising the income from its possession of Bombay for funding its reproduction of capital. Hence, it saw to it that income from Bombay was increased. It may, therefore, be noted that in spite of the claim by the British authorities that the agreement agreed upon at the Aungier's Convention of 1674, though not signed and ratified by the Company seems to have been regarded valid and acted upon. It was, in fact, neither strictly followed nor acted upon by the Court of Directors of the Company. The Court was invariably interested in raising more and more income from lands on the island of Bombay through observation or through default of the principles and contents of the agreement of the Aungier's Convention.

In 1679-80, within half a decade of the Aungier's Convention, the Court of Directors wrote to the Surat Council to survey all Company's lands in Bombay and let them on leases for a term of years on a definite annual rental. In the same letter it was ordered that "all arable land on the island be surveyed, the producer of each to be calculated, the value of the quarter share due to the Company may be ascertained. These were to be farmed out for a term of years to avoid the collecting rent in land yearly. It has got to be noted here that faming out land was the system of creating new landlord as farmers who were to be intermediaries between the Company and the real cultivators, and exploit the later. Besides, in the same year (1679-80) the houses were ordered to be valued and a proportionate tax to be imposed on each. As a consequence by 1688 apart from a tonnage fee on all ships and an increase in the duty charges on imports, a quit-rent was levied on all houses as follows: 2 shillings and 5 penes on a great house, one shilling and 6 penes on a middling house and one shilling on a small house per annum.

In the meanwhile, Captain Richard Keigwig led a revolt of soldiers during 1683-84 and Siddi's attacked Bombay during 1674 and 1689-90. The mutiny of the English soldiers and Siddi's attacks shook awfully the Company's Government over Bombay. These disturbances accompanied with plague epidemic resulted in the migration of a large number of people from Bombay and as a consequence depopulation of the island took place. Many estates were left tenantless and many fields uncultivated. As Portuguese in general and Jesuits in particular acted hostile to the Company and collaborated with the Siddi's during their attacks on Bombay all the lands and properties of the Portuguese, particularly of Jesuits, were confiscated in 1791.[29] The Court of Directors wrote to Surat and Bombay on 1st May 1693: "Stick to all confiscated estates, but as to the manner sort of Portuguese use some sort of consideration to restore to the island again with working inhabitants, so that you may admit such to their own Residencies' and estates after condemnation, they paying for the future annually half the fruits of their Oarts or grounds, at our first receiving the island of the Crown they ought to have paid us only the fourth part of their fruits and fourth for bribes to the then English Deputy Governor was commuted into a money rent at a great under-valuation to the Company's loss ever since." The point to remember here is that Court of Directors referred to the matter in consideration at the time of its possession of island and not to what was agreed upon on the matter in the agreement at the Aungier's Convention of 1674. However, in compliance to the order of the Court of Directors, the Bombay Council wrote to the Court on 3rd October 1694. "the value was set on Oarts is 5 × 5, a tree with the common valuation between a buyer and seller, they esteeming a tree to be worth 1/9, a year which is ten years, purchase, the constant valuation of land here (was on money being at 12 percent interest) is 5 × 5 and all batty grounds we have valued at 20 × 5 per Mora, which is 20 × 5 per annum." This indicates that Siddi attacks resulted not only in creation of a new class of tenants who held land on leases but also in new valuation of Oarts, trees and lands with a view to increasing the revenue of the Honourable Company.

In the meanwhile, the Company collected a head tax from every Koli for the liberty of fishing and following other occupations. The head money paid by every Koli was Rs. 3 to 4 a year. It w. . especially for those who followed callings other than fishing. Palanquin paid the same as fishing Kolis. The question here is as to why the Company charged a tax from the Kolis opting for any other occupation than fishing. Does it not mean that the Company believed in the natives sticking to their traditional occupation, and restricted all change of occupation by them? This, however, might not have been the reason, what, therefore might have been the reason was the Company's avarice to make money for reason or no reason. The Company further charged half the produce of salt made by persons on ports belonging to the Company, and it also collected tributes from Bhandaris for drawing. Toddy from the Company's trees. In this way there were numerous items connected on which the Company levied taxes as a part of land revenue, the justification for which being nothing but the Company's capitalistic greed to get money for investment in its enterprise in England. The Company, indeed, wanted fund for the production of capital in England no matter that involved maintaining or reverting to production relations to slavery or feudal of the native population of its possession like Bombay. In such a policy of the Company can be found the reason for the lopsided development of the relations of productions, in land tenures on the island of Bombay during the rule of the Company.

A study of the development of the land relations on the island of Bombay since the Aungier's Convention indicates that the Honourable Company did not strictly observe what was agreed upon. The payment with regard to the pension tenure, which originated during the Portuguese period, dates back from Aungier's agreement. This payment commuted in consideration of the payment every year of 20,000 xeraphins (Rs. 13,850). Whatever right the Company possessed over the estates which were in a state of cultivation and which were in consequence acknowledged by that instrument to be freehold property, under a reservation, however, of a claim of military services of the inhabitants.[30] The above mentioned sum was determined from an account, taken in 1672 of true value of the annual produce of all the land, which was considered to be worth 80,000 xeraphins of which 20,000 xeraphins being one-fourth were to be paid annually to the Company.

In 1758, the Company introduced a tax of 10 percent in the produce of landed estate to meet "the prodigious expenses and to build fortification and other works for the security of inhabitants."[31] Actually, speaking the Honourable Richard Benchier, the then Governor of Bombay, while introducing this tax had told the citizens of Bombay that the said tax was imposed with a view to raising money for maintaining war with the French, and had promised that they would be relieved of the same as soon as that war was over. The said tax brought to the Company an extra income of Rs. 58,263-1-40 but the official objections were raised on the ground that the said amount was collected by under-valuation of estates; hence an order was issued for proper valuation and larger collection thereof.

It is interesting to note that when in 1774 the inhabitants of Bombay prayed for abolition of this tax, reminding the Honourable Company what the Governor of Bombay had promised at the time of the imposition of this tax, the Court of Directors refused to accept the plea of the inhabitants and in a letter dated 12th April 1775 wrote "As our fortifications are far from being completed, they cannot consent to relinquish the tax laid upon the landed estates in 1758, which was designed as an aid to the Company in the erecting of those fortifications." Thus, the Company not only violated the agreement made at the Aungier Convention but it did not honour the promise made by its Governor to the inhabitants of Bombay.

Introduction of Quit-rent

The Honourable Company's capitalist avarice can be observed from its another device to make money from the land in Bombay by introducing quit-rent. It originated in a letter to the Bombay Council by the Court of Directors. It said "Remember your promise to improve the ground rents within the city walls by the methods therein specified of letting leased renewable or by fines or quit rents or whatever the way you should judge most of our interest. The consideration of our prodigious charge and the people's protection and liberties are, if rightly managed, very cogent argument to convince everyone why that ground ought to be valued higher than if otherwise would be." It is worth marking out how the Court of Directors often talked about its 'Prodigious Charges', 'the people's protection and liberties' and soon to raise income from the lands in the City and Island of Bombay and that too without caring for Mr. Aungier's commitment to the agreement of the Convention of 1674. It is further amusing to note that the Court instructed its representatives in Bombay to raise more money by whatever the means which might be renewable leases or fines or quit rent and for which it wanted its representatives in Bombay to rightly manage the cogent argument bringing home to the people of Bombay Company's prodigious charges towards protection of their lives, properties and liberties. This reminds one, the debate in the British Parliament on the question as to whether or not do Britain export goods to India to balance the surplus import from India to the tune of £ 3,700,000 in 1786. The official reply was that it was not necessary to cover the imports from India by exports to that country to the same amount because the British made up surplus of import from India by exporting 'good government' of India.[32]

End of Feudal Tenure and Beginning of Capitalist Tenure

In pursuance of the order of the Court of Directors to improve, the ground rents within the city walls a tax or a quit-rent was imposed in 1718 on all lands and house owners within town walls. This tax, it is remarked, changed the ancient constitution of the island by commuting military services, for a quit-rent though this was applicable to the people living within the town walls. While commenting on this tax the compiler of Gazetteer of Bombay City and Island, as stated back, remarks "this tax may be said to have substituted a money charge for the liability to military service, and ended the feudal tenure."[33] But at a different place in a footnote the same compiler questions and answers his above mentioned statement as follows:

> "But of Aungier's Convention reserved personal service of tenant in every part of the island, it is not apparent how the introduction of quit-rent on the lands in the fort alone redeemed it possibly the levy of this rent in the fort was sufficient to raise a military in times of war."[34]

It may, however, be observed that the above mentioned answer to the question therein of quit-rent is not accurate. Actually speaking the Honourable Company was simply interested in increasing its income by any excuse, and it was not at all the concern whether the levy of that tax on the land within the town walls was sufficient to raise a military or not in times of war. This is proved from the fact that when several of the inhabitants built houses without the town walls or outside the town walls, a proclamation was at once issued reducing the quit-rent to one-half and extending it to all houses within the cannon shot of the town walls.[35]

In the meanwhile, this rent was levied on rates being at variance between the English inhabitants and the Indian inhabitants and in the course of time it was equalized for the both. However the Honourable Company went on increasing this rent indicating its capitalistic greed for more and more income from the lands in Bombay. It is needless to state that the Honourable Company did try for the same as the Town Committee in 1837 opined that the Government had power to alter the rent on these lands it required, and the same was done when the British Crown took over the control of India from the Honourable Company after and, as a consequence of, the revolt of 1857.

Toka Land Tenure and Company's Policy

The case of the Toka land tenure under the Company's rule further indicate how the Company acquired much of this type of land and attempted to increase its income from it – Toka lands, originally denoting government grounds under cultivation on payment of Toka or share of produce, computed later on into money payment annually, were situated on the north-east of the island from Sion to Sewri.[36] They comprised 1489 thousand and 764 square yards. The early history of these lands shows that the Kunbis or tenants who cultivated these lands could be removed at the pleasure of the government. The right of the proprietorship of these lands were founded on the fact that all cultivated and waste lands excepting such as by constitution of proprietorship of these lands were founded on the fact that all cultivated and waste lands excepting such as by constitution of the island was appendage of the cultivated portion as pasturage ground, were at the date of Aungier's Convention Crown lands, which as the time went on were let out for cultivation to the 'Kunbis, the produce being equally divided between the Company and the tenants, a reasonable allowance always made in bad seasons. [37] The right of the Company on these lands, as shown in the foregoing pages, is quite doubtful. The Company confiscated the Jesuits land in 1692 and Rama Kamati's property in 1720 and made money through auctioning these lands for 7 years. This was done in 1751 as follows: The batty grounds in Parel were let for 2,605, in Sion for Rs. 1,300, in Dharavi for Rs. 273, in Matunga for Rs. 1,965, in Wadala for Rs. 1,761, in Naigaon for Rs. 982, in Bomnolly for Rs. 530, and in Mahim and Worli for Rs. 144, the total amount being Rs. 9560.[38] Thus the company added to its income Rs. 1,366-9-2 $^{5/7}$ annually.

Foras Land Tenure

The word Foras is derived from the Portuguese word 'Foro' which meant rent. It is not very clear in what form and how much this type of rent was charged by the Portuguese though this type of tenure did exist in some form during the Portuguese rule of Bombay. The Company, however, introduced a distinct Foras land tenure. During Company's rule, Foras was a particular rent paid by a cultivator or a person permitted to occupy a ground for the purpose of improving it, but without any lease or grant by which he could maintain possession during the continuance of his term.[39]

The Foras lands were also known as 'Salt Batty' grounds as these had been reclaimed from the sea, "which traversed the island in different directions, finding outlets for itself at Back bay, Mazagaon, and other parts and dividing Bombay into a cluster of island."[40] The Foras lands or salt batty grounds were of two types the old batty grounds and the new batty grounds. The old batty grounds were situated between Sion and Mahim having reclaimed from the sea by construction of a vellard, and the new batty grounds were located near Mahalaxmi having been recovered from the sea by means of a Hornby vellard constructed in 1770. In the beginning of the 18th Century, the Kunbis or cultivators were encouraged in the above areas to develop Foras lands free of rents for a number of years but later on the Company began to claim some rent on the ground that it had constructed the vellards at great expense to facilitate the reclamation of these lands. The question here arises as to whether the Company constructed the vellards for the reclamation of land by and for the cultivators or for some other purpose. Actually speaking the Company constructed them for many purposes such as linking of different parts of Islands for smooth administration, better transport and greater trades-local as well as inland. The Government of Bombay, in a letter, dated 19th April 1820, with reference to the Beach Candy vellard point out "The work in question was built not exclusively for the security of the salt batty grounds though that description of land arose out of its construction, but for the general improvement of island."[41]

The Company, however, was inclined to put forth any, proper or improper, plea for making some income from Foras land cultivators. In 1740, the Company notified to farm out these lands (Foras lands) in parcels or whole at the so-called land rate of 4 reas per burga (60 square yards). Farming out of lands itself marks a capitalistic endeavor to create landlord or land owner over and above the cultivators for the sake of some more income. Not satisfied with the rent of only 4 reas per burga the Company raised it from 4 reas to 6 reas in 1774 and to 9 reas in 1748 under the pretext of new measurement, having been taken by them. It is difficult to understand how measurement causes fresh valuation of Foras land for raising the rent from 4 to 9 reas. It is indeed, quite interesting to mark that the Honorable Company often increased the rent in the name of either fresh measurement or uniform rate as, for instance, the Dharavi lands which were also reclaimed from the sea shore, 10 and 15 reas per burgas, depending upon the quality of lands, but in 1748 uniform rent was raised to 15 reas per burga.[42] The question is why 15 reas per burga in the name of uniform rate, why not 10 reas or 12½ reas?

The Foras land tenure in course of time led to long legal dispute between the Company's Government in Bombay and the tenants of that category of land but what is pertinent to note is that the Honourable Company always tried to increase its collection from this type of otherwise free or nominal land tenure, the Company's income for instance, being Rs. 1,492 from the 'salt batty' grounds and Rs. 7,748 from 'batty' grounds as early as 1735-36.[43]

Strangely enough, in tune with the Honourable Company's avarice for more income Mr. Munroe in 1812 submitted a report pleading that the Company should reap some further benefit from the Foras lands and later on, he wrote: "If I am allowed to offer our opinion on what has been stated in regard to an equitable assessment on the new and old salt batty ground, I would respectfully recommend that it be assessed at the rate of 5¾ Adolis per burga, which will give 7 'Shers', one 'tipree'. One third of a 'Tipree' will yield to the government in a favorable season (supposing the salt batty Toka to be annually fixed at the moderate rate of Rs. 21 per; muda'). Rs. 13,735-0-17 more than the Company's present annual revenue from these grounds which amount to Rs. 3,912-1-06,"[44] It was no surprise that the Government of Bombay accepted Mr.

Munroe's recommendations and notified on 1st November 1813 that the rent of the new and old batty grounds was to be increased.

The case was, however, submitted for Mr. Advocate General Mocklin's opinion on two inter-related questions. *First,* whether the Government possessed the right of increasing the rent of salt batty grounds, etc. and *second,* whether in the event of the proprietors refusing to pay the increased rent the Government could resume possession of this description of property. The Advocate-General's reply was that the native land holders of Bombay of every denomination were originally invited to settle on the island under the idea that the land allotted to them was in perpetuity, hence "The Government had not either the right to increase the rent or resume the land at their pleasures." It seems another Advocate-General Mr. Tripeland had given his opinion contrary to that of Mr. Mocklin. The Court of Directors gave its judgement in favour of the opinion of Mr.Tripeland but Sir James Mackintosh made an observation "tending to support the view of the subject taken by Mr. Mocklin," Hence the matter was referred to the Honourable Court of Directors of the Company. The Court agreed to permit making of the grants of lands to the land holders in perpetuity but warned the local government as follows:

> "In doing this, you will be careful to receive the present rents, and annex a condition for grantee's assuming the repairs of the vellard, and we direct you to explicitly guard against the possibility of their this conception that their lands are to be exempted from any taxes or assessment now payable for public purposes, general or local, or which it may be deemed proper hereafter to impose upon landed property or occupation."[45]

Thus, the Honourable Company again inter-alia raised the question of vellard on the pretext for charging rent and increasing the same or leaving the repairs of vellard to the landholders in case they opposed the increasing of rent and soon the matter of the repairs of vellards however, created difficulties for the local government, which in its letter dated the 19th April 1920, wrote to the Court of Directors as under:

> "We have the honour to report the impracticability of giving effect to your Honourable Court's commands in regard to the grant in perpetuity directed to be made to the several holders of salt batty ground until a survey of the whole land of that description of property shall have been completed. In the meantime, we beg to call your Honourable Court's attention to the observations of the collector on the part of your orders, which more immediately relate to the Beach Candy vellard. The work in question was built not exclusively for the security of the salt batty ground though that description of land arose out of its construction, but for general improvement of the island. The whole revenue from the new and old salt batty ground amount to about Rs. 4,000 being assessed at different rates, from 6, 7 and 9 to 14 reas per burga of 64 square yards. The expense of keeping the vellard in repair may be taken at about Rs. 1,500 per annum, and if that expense be thrown upon the proprietors it will land to an advance annually 5 percent. Upon the present rent which we do not imagine that your Honourable Court intended to impose on this particular description of property for the preservation of the work equally beneficial to other inhabitants of the island, and particularly to the Fazindari and proprietors of ground situated on the low part of the island. The liberal intention of your Honourable Court of issuing grants in perpetuity in favors of these lands might be less exceptionally carried in effect by fixing the rents for the future at the highest of the existing rates, namely 14 reas the 'burga' and by inserting a charge stipulating that in the event of any portion being hereafter required either for military cantonment or any other public purpose, compensation shall be made to the owners for the value of the improvement in building, trees, wells and tanks to be ascertained by a jury and not of the soil itself. We would however prefer that this arrangement should be postponed until the survey of the island shall have been completed."[46]

In 1827, Mr. Tate carried out a survey of Foras lands but no measures were taken up to the year 1836 towards making the grants in perpetuity as suggested by the Court of Directors or the modifications of that suggested by the Government of Bombay. In the meanwhile in 1836, the project of Grant Road, which was to cover the Foras land, again revived the question whether or not the Kunbis or cultivators possessed rights on such lands in perpetuity, and hence dispose them as building ground without the sanction of the government. The Town Committee opined that the Government possessed 'an undoubted and indefeasible rights' on this description of land and proposed that the whole of the Foras grounds under cultivation to the south of the Bellasis Road should be taken over by the Government by paying the compensation at the rate of 5 years 'Foras' and the holders of land in that area should be offered gratis building site, the frontage and square contents of which should bear same proportion say 1120th to the quantities of such grounds. The Committee further proposed that "the holders of the Foras lands to the north and East Bellasis Road should for the future be debarred from using or disposing of any part thereof for building grounds without the sanction of Government, any violation of this rule to subject the defending party to the forfeiture of his property."[47]

Surprisingly, the Committee further suggested to raise the rents of the Foras lands used for cultivation.[48] On the above mentioned submission of the Town Committee, the Government of Bombay in December 1837 opined that the resumption of the Foras lands from their holders "without such a value of the property as with building sites gratis in other parts of the island would be considered just equivalent."[49] Moreover, it said, such an act would be unpopular. It was, however, pointed out that the rights of the Government should be reserved to resume the above referred lands for "roads, streets or government buildings, or other public purpose, paying only the value of any buildings thereon."[50] Such being the view on the matter in dispute when in 1838 the work for construction of Grant Road was commenced on the land of the above mentioned disputed description without any compensation, the land-holders did not at all complain as that was for the expressed public benefit.

The matter in regard to the controversy referred above would have rested there if the capitalist-mined Government of Bombay of the capitalistic enterprise as the East India company had not resumed some plots near the Race-course, then adjacent to Byculla, for the purpose of stacking hay of private individuals, the private capitalist, without paying any compensation. This action of the local government resulted in a memorial land-holders of that description for the restoration of their rights on these lands at the ancient rate of taxation, as they were evicted from their lands not for public benefit but for the benefit of private individuals the owners of hay.[51] The memorial was sent to the Advocate-General Mr. Lemesurier for his opinion who opined that the government had rights neither to resume the lands of that description not to increase the rent thereof. On this opinion of the Advocate-General, the local government passed an order on the 4th of April 1844 with the effect that it would not resume the lands of that description except for public utility and that too without paying any compensation and it would not raise the existing rate of assessment.[52]

The Government of Bombay, however, proposed *(i)* That a careful survey should be made of the actual state of all lands in question. *(ii)* That a prospective plan of roads, streets, drains, tanks and other public works suited to the wants of the population which might ultimately be located on these lands should then be laid down. *(iii)* That a code of rules should be drawn up for regulating the erection of buildings in the district in question with a view to insure uniformity of construction and to provide for all points effecting the public health convenience and safety. This proposal was submitted to the Court of Directors of the Company who in their dispatch No. 28 of 10th November 1844 approved the proposal in general but remarked that the only tax on assessment leviable then or thereafter was to be paid by the holders of landed property or occupation in general.

A plan in this regard indicating the proposed roads, etc., was prepared by the chief engineer in consultation with the Collector and the Municipal authorities, and approved by Court of Directors. The land holder when communicated about this plan held a few meetings among themselves and majority of them, in spite of lack of unanimity expressed agreement to the following arrangement :

(i) That the ground required for roads, etc., should be delivered to the government, the holders thereof being compensated at the rates determined by a committee of the principal landholders.

(ii) That a fund should be raised by means of a contribution from all Foras land-holders, proportioned to the quantity of land. This was, however, opposed by a group of Foras land-holders. Thereafter a few other suggestions were made and ultimately the Foras Act VI was passed on the 6th June 1851 in this regard.

The aforesaid Act, passed by the Legislative Council of India while confirming the holders in their possession accompanied two plans as follows. The lands comprised in the plan No.1 were given to the persons who held the same respectively as the immediate rent payers to the Company, subject to the rates then severally payable in respect of those lands, and the lands comprised in plan No. 2 were vested in Government from 1st July 1851 free from all rights for the purpose of construction of roads, etc.[53] A committee appointed on the 25th July 1851 to carry out the provisions of the Foras Act fixed different rates of compensation according to locality as under[54]:

For lands from Khetwadi to Central	Rs. 10 Per Burga
For lands from Central Circle to Tardeo	Rs. 7 Per Burga
For lands from Corner near Gowalia Tank to the Circle	Rs. 16½ Per Burga
For lands from Circle to new Town	Rs. 12 Per Burga
For lands from Bellasis to Phippi's Oart	Rs. 2 to 6 Per Burga
For lands from Phippi's Oart to Sion Northwards from	Rs. 1 to 2 Per Burga

Thus, the prolonged controversy about the Foras lands was settled but even the Company under the pretext of the Foras lands increased its income from this description of land. The total receipt from various landholders of the Foras lands from 12th April 1852 to 5th September 1853 amounted to Rs. 57,557, the sum being almost twenty times more than what was collected from this description of land in 1812 and this also being four times more than what in 1812 Mr. Munroe had proposed it to be, which had, however, set in the controversy regarding this kind of tenure, described in the foregoing pages. It seems that the high and rocky grounds in Mahim were not used for cultivation as there is no mention in the contemporary documents all out any tenure regarding such lands. It was the ever-increasing greed of the Honourable Company to put in use even such lands for raising some income from them. The Company introduced what was known as Kurleet tenure through letting out high and rocky grounds in some parts of the Mahim districts for cultivation. Although the Gazetteer of Bombay City and Island casually remarks that the cultivators of such grounds paid 'petty tribute' to the government.[55] The fact indicates that the cultivators of such grounds had to pay one third of the produce as tax to the Company. The question is whether or not one-third of the produce of any ground can be treated as 'petty tribute.'

The company introduced the Inami land tenure in 1783 when on recommendation of Sir Edward Hughes K. B. Commander-In-Chief of His Majesty's ship in India, the Company granted free of charge certain batty grounds in the district of Parel to the Parsi Master Builder Maneckji and Bomanji Lawji and their two sons-Framji and Jamshedji Lawji. This grant was made in recognition of services of that family in refitting His Majesty's squadron. The grant was, however, ratified and confirmed by the Court of Directors, after 12 years, on the 20th April 1795. The second such grant was made in 1821 on the application of Jamshedji Bomanji for the grant of cultivated lands yielding an annual rent of Rs. 6,000. In the meanwhile it appears the applicant expired as the letter of the Secretary to the Government dated 12th September States that

"The grants should be made by transferring to the heirs of Jamshedjee's the revenue payable to the government under a formal engagement that the present assessment should not be increased and securing the Curmbees the right of cultivation and all such other privileges as they may be entitled to by the constitution of the island and under stipulation that in the event of the usual assessment being increased or any other modification introduced in the existing revenue system of the island by the authority of the government, the same shall have operation within the village to be granted."[56]

The Collector replied this letter by stating that the Company's salt batty grounds produced a revenue yearly of Rs. 4,026-0-33 and the sweet batty grounds yielded annually Rs. 9,678 but out of them there were three, *viz.*, Matunga, Sion and Dharavi, whose amount was yearly Rs. 3,448 that sum deducted for six villages an annual rent of Rs. 6,226 and then he pointed out that he proposed to take out three villages out of six in case the Government or the Artillery at any further period required more grounds at Matunga or at Sion and Dharavi. To this the Secretary to the government of Bombay on 20th October 1821 replied as follows :

> "I am directed by the Honourable Governor in Council to acknowledge receipt of your letter dated 10th the ultimo and to inform you that lands yielding an annual rent of Rs. 4,000 will be granted to the family of late Jamshedji Bomanji on the island of Salsette... Nawroji having requested that the remainder of the grant. *viz.*, Rs. 2,000 per annum may be assigned in paddy lands on the island of Bombay, the Honourable Governor in Council has been pleased to comply with the request subject to the confirmation of the Honourable Court of Directors under the conditions specified in my letter of the 12th of the last month, you will be pleased to adopt the necessary measures for putting the family in possession of the land accordingly in such manner as may be agreeable to them."

In January 1822, the government authorized the Collector to put Nawroji Jamshedji in possession of the batty grounds in the village of Parel, Naigaon, Sion and in the Kasba of Mahim. On the 2nd February 1822, Nawroji Jamshedji signed a declaration. On October 1824, Nawroji Jamshedji applied to the Government for a formal deed of gift or Sanad, which was drawn up in the name of Nawroji Jamshedji, Mancherji Jamshedji and Dossabhoy Jamshedji, sole heirs and representatives of Jamshedji Bomanji, enabling them to collect and receive revenue of the gifted lands and enjoy the same as their own sole and absolute property.

In 1854, Nawroji Jamshedji Wadia sent a petition to the local government praying as follows. "Your memorialist beg to represent that he receives the revenue of two villages in Salsette (Illaparia and Jhoo) which now yields the annual sum of Rs. 4,711 out of which 711 your memorialist refunds to the government being the surplus amount of the revenue of the said two villages, and which villages are allowed in Inam to your memorialist, with the net stipulated amount of Rs. 4,000 per annum. That your memorialist further begs to state that he also receives the produce of an Inam land at Sion, in Bombay, which yields Rs. 605 annually, and which being intermixed with government land makes it difficult for collecting the revenue. He, therefore, prays that he may be allowed to exchange the produce of the land at Sion with the above village in Salsette, *viz.*, that he may be allowed to retain the sum of Rs. 311, the surplus revenue of the two villages of Illapuria and Jhoo, in return for which the Government may be pleased to retain the revenue of the land at Sion, the deficiency of Rs. 106 in the revenue of the Sion land your memorialist will thankfully pay at whatever valuation Government may think it fair to receive from your memorialist."

The Collector with reference to the above mentioned memorial replied on 31st March 1855 as under:

> "If government were to take back this (Sion) land there would of course be a small addition to the work to be performed by the establishment of this office involving however no increase of expense except perhaps the pay of

an extra peon for three months in the year say Rs. 18/- per annum. During the last twenty years remission of token assessment have been allowed in consequence of partial failure of crops as under. In 1835-36, to the extent of about one-third, in 1837 one-third, in 1838 two-third in 1842 one-half, in 1845 one-half, in 1852 one-half." He further stated: "Had the lands in Sion of which Nawroji Jamshedji receives the Toka been held by government the sums which cultivators in these years would have aggregated Rs. 1511-4-0 or an average of 20 years Rs. 75-8-0 per annum. If, therefore, the right of Honourable Governor in Council should be disposed to comply with Nawroji Jamshedjee's application as an act of grace, I am of the opinion that these should be deducted from the amount of Toka assessment on account of charges of collection of Rs. 18 and for probable remission of Rs. 75, and the land taken over as equivalent only to Rs. 511 per annum (Rs. 604-8-0, Rs. 93-8-0). The net proceeds are not likely to be much above or below this sum on an average of years."

The Goverrtment then in May 1855 passed orders to make exchange requested by Nawroji Jamshedji taking the exchangeable value of his land at Sion to be Rs. 511 per annum on condition that the difference between this sum and the Koli rental paid by him should be made good to the Collector of Thana. The terms having been accepted by Nawroji Jamshedji, a deed of exchange was drawn up and executed by the parties. The Sion lands thus reverted to the Government and were termed to be held by the tenants on the Toka tenure. The Third grant made to Khan Bahadur Jamshedji Dhunjibhai Wadia belongs to 1905, hence not to be discussed as having beyond the scope of this study.

The Company also introduced lease tenure in Bombay which involved the farming of lease under various conditions and terms verifying from 21 to 999 years. The leases during the rule of the East India Company were

(*i*) Mazgaon or Byculla leases,

(*ii*) Colaba leases,

(iii) Kamathipura leases,

(iv) the leases on the verge of the Esplanade, and

(v) Bombay leases.

The Mazgaon or Byculla leases belong to the period from 1758 to 1796.

There were leases for the term of 99 years, some being renewable and some not renewable. In addition to the annual rents the leases were to pay a certain fine every 21 years. The Colaba leases belonged to the year 1894. This was done on a report of Committee consisting of the Collector of Bombay, the revenue surveyor and the Company's solicitor which was appointed in August 1822 to consider the matter of leases of the lands in Colaba. The Committee's recommendation contained *(a)* That the lands outside the limits of the military regulations of 1793, outside the limit of the military cantonment could be granted on leases and *(b)* That the leases should be granted to the occupants of those lands for 21 years, renewable upon payment of a fine of Rs. 100 at a uniform ground rent of 3 reas per square yard per annum. The Government accepted the Committee's recommendations. However, in 1836 the Court of Directors desired that the ground on the island of Colaba should be retained by the government in its own possession. The Government of Bombay pointed out difficulties in doing so and proposed that the vacant places on that island should be granted to the private individuals on payment of the established ground rent of 6 pies per square yard with right of resumption. This was approved by the Court of Directors in May 1838. There appeared two kinds of leases, renewable every 21 years. The one permanent paying 3 reas per square yard and the other resumable which required paying 6 pies per square yard. There were the Kamathipura leases, most probably belonging to the year 1844. The form of the leases was settled in consultation with the Advocate General in 1846 when it was approved also. These leases for, were 21 years' leases, renewable at revised rents. However, the practice of leasing was different as the lands were put to public auction and leased to the highest bidders, the rents at the outset being reserved at 6 pies per square yard.

The leases on the verge of the Esplanade belonged to the year 1855 as follows. The local government authorized by the Court of Directors of the irregular plots of grounds in village of Esplanade in manner best calculated to promote the public interest. These irregular plots were made to certain parties in 1835 on condition that no permanent structures but simply wooden should be built and the ground should be handed over to the Government as and when required without any compensation. In 1851, it was discovered that permanent structures were erected on some of these plots in question. In September 1853 the Collector reported to the government the occupant had surrendered lands to him by writing which was considered to give to the Government legal possession thereof. The Collector in the same letter further recommended that the lands in question might let in terms which would admit of their being occupied by permanent buildings. This envisaged the process of leasing out those lands and a form of lease was devised and after approval of the government, the lands were sold by auction to the highest bidders.

The above referred developments in regard to the land relations in City and Island of Bombay during few decades of the seventeenth century (*viz.*, from 1668 to 1700), throughout eighteenth century and by the middle of the nineteenth century indicate the process of transformation of feudal land to semi-feudal land and semi-capitalist land to capitalist land.

REFERENCES

1. V.I. Lenin: Collected works Vol. I, Moscow, 1963, p., 136.
2. V.I. Povlov: Historical Premises for India's Transition to Capitalism, p. 7.
3. *Ibid.*, pp. 9-10.
4. *Ibid.*
5. Gazetteer of Bombay City and Island, Vol. II, p. 32.
6. The circumstances entailed the Sultan being apprehensive of the power of the Mughal Emperors and his observations of the

successes obtained by Portuguese arms; hence desire to enlist their aid as need.

7. There also existed a minor tenure known as Arrendamento signifying the annual letting or renting of land for a fixed sum in cash or kind.

8. According to the G.B.C.I. (vol. II, p. 32) the identity of Mestro Diogo is doubtful but he may conceivably have been either Diogo de Barba, an evangelist and the founder of the first catechetical school in Bassein, or Diogo da Silvera a cousin of Heitor da Silveira

9. Garcia da Orta was honorary physician of King Joao III.

10. G.B.C.I., Vol. II, pp. 36-37.

11. *Ibid.*

12. *Ibid*, p. 40.

13. G.B.C.I., *Op cit.*, Vol. II, p. 38-9.

14. S.M.Edwardes, Rise of Bombay: A Retrospect. (Bombay, 1902).

15. G.B.C.I., Vol. II, pp. 44-5.

16. Gerson Da Cunha – Origin of Bombay (1900), p. 215.

17. G.B.C.I., Vol. II, p. 308.

18. *Ibid*, p. 309.

19. Maharashtra State Gazetteer- Greater Bombay District, Vol. II, p. 16.

20. G.B.C.I., Vol. II, p. 356.

21. *Ibid.*, Vol. I, p. 64.

22. *Ibid.*, Vol. II, p. 310.

23. The reference is about the bourgeoisie anti-feudal revolution in England during 1641-53.

24. Karl Marx : Capital, Vol. I, p. 672.

25. The so called representatives of the people of Bombay were generally a small number of Portuguese landlords and land-holders.

26. G.B.C.I., Vol. II, pp. 315–18.

27. *Ibid.*, pp. 318-19, general administration report 1901-2, p. 47.

28. *Ibid.*, p. 347.

29. At the time of the cession of the island to the British Crown, the Jesuits were the sole possessors of Parel, Vadala and Sion. These properties of Jesuit were confiscated in 1791.
30. G.B.C.I., Vol. II, p. 335.
31. *Ibid.*, p. 336.
32. British Parliamentary Papers, 1927, 1922, 1926.
33. *Ibid.*, p. 321.
34. *Ibid.*
35. Government Consultation of 30th Sept. 1720, G.B.C.I., Vol. II, p. 321.
36. G.B.C.I., Vol. II, p. 347.
37. *Ibid.*, p. 348.
38. *Ibid.*, p. 349.
39. *Ibid.*, p. 358.
40. *Ibid.*
41. *Ibid.*, p. 339.
42. *Ibid.*, p. 359.
43. *Ibid.*, p. 441.
44. *Ibid.*
45. *Ibid.*, p. 366.
46. *Ibid.*, pp. 366-67.
47. *Ibid.*
48. *Ibid.*, p. 369.
49. *Ibid.*
50. *Ibid.*
51. *Ibid.*, p. 370.
52. *Ibid.*, p. 371.
53. *Ibid.*, p. 373.
54. *Ibid.*
55. *Ibid.*, p. 358.
56. *Ibid.*, p. 375.

3

Mercantilism, Moneylending and Speculation

(17th and 18th Century)

It is a well known fact that Bombay came in the hands of British King Charles II as part of dowry through his marriage with the Portuguese Princes Catherine the Braganza in the year 1661. After seven years the island was given to East India Company on a nominal rent of £ 10 annually. This was a very timely acquisition for Company because their main factory at Surat had come to be threatened by the Marathas. Therefore, when the Company acquired the island it not only got a safer place to defend itself but also got an excellent harbor which could be of very much useful for trading and commercial activities in spite of its unhealthy climate. The East India Company got transferred its main factory to Surat from Bombay in 1687 and since then it made every effort to develop the island as its commercial and political centre. The efforts of the Company bore fruit and by the middle of the 18th century Bombay had become the emporium of Persia, Arabia and the Western part of India where the manufacture and produce of the world were to be readily procured.[1] At the time of British acquisition of Island from Portuguese, the island was inhabited by ancient Kolis, few Portuguese families and servants of British government and Company.[2]

By the 18th century, the importance of Gujarat ports

declined on account of feudal anarchy and decline in foreign trade. Hence the merchants of Gujarat started moving to Bombay at the instance of English factors that needed local intermediaries to carry out their trading business with the districts adjacent to Bombay Island which were in the hands of the Marathas. Thus the need of the East India Company afforded itself to give invitation to the merchants to settle on Bombay Island on most favored conditions. As early as 1671 when Surat Banias were asked by the Company to move to Bombay they demanded that the Company should grant them a number of priviledges.[3] It was in this way that the Banias from Surat (Neema Parekh) and Diu made the island their home on invitation of the Company and they were followed by Armenians (Khoja Karakuz, Khoja Minaz and Khoja Delaune) and lastly by Parsis.[4] All these communities played an important role in the commercial development of Bombay during the 17th and 18th century.

The Kapol Banias came from Gogha and Surat with their leader Seth Rupji Dhanji about the year 1756. The Bhatias came from Kathiawar and Cutch about the beginning of the 19th century and with an object of trade they sailed to Zanzibar, Muscat, Japan and China but did not go to Europe and America because of prohibition by their religion to travel by sea.[5] The prominent men of this community in the 70's and 80's of the 18th century were Sheth Mangal Das Nathubhai, Sheth Sir Harkison Das Narottam Das and Sheth Varjivan Das who built Madhav Baug Temple.[6]

A very close commercial link developed between the English and Parsi merchants. The Parsis are descendants of Zorastrains who fled from Iran on account of their persecution at the hands of Mohammadans. Firstly they arrived at Sanjan in the middle of 8th century which is some 94 miles north of Bombay, at the close of seaboard of Gujarat in a district which stretched for forty miles along the coast and twenty miles inland.[7] Their long stay in Gujarat had made them to establish close connections with the economic, political and cultural life of the people of Gujarat. They had even adopted the Gujarati language as their mother tongue. However they maintained their separate identity by not marrying with another community. Only the caste system and religion had prevented their complete assimilation otherwise they were also Guajaratis as they spoke the Gujarati language.[8]

It would be incorrect to think that commerce has always been the only occupation of the Parsis. In fact they worked as agriculturists, supplied the sailor with timber and water and a few of them even worked as weavers. They also worked as tobacco growers, prepared palm wine and practiced commerce, money changing and handicrafts. The forefathers of Peston Jahangir, the Bombay capitalist born in 1831, received from the great Mughals a Jagir near Surat and the titles Nekshant Khan and Jabiar Khan.[9] Prominent representatives of the Indian Middle class such as Dadabhai Nauroji and Tata are descendants of landowners. Chand Kamadin an ancestor of Nauroji nine generations removed won by his skill as perfumer, secured the favour of the beautiful Nurjahan, the wife of Jahangir and in 1618 was granted 100 bighas of land free of tax. The Parsis were therefore not restricted in their profession by religious prohibitions of feudal India. From early times Parsis established connections as brokers with European traders. A remarkable feature to be noted about the Parsis is that their traditional occupations were not connected with trading or finance. In the accounts of the 17th century travelers, they are noticed chiefly as artisans, carpenters, weavers, etc. Their prominence in Bombay was also established in the first instance through their ship building activity. Though they later became dominant trading and financing community like other Gujarat communities, their original artisan background was an important feature that deserves notice.[10] After the European merchants came to India; brokerage became the main occupation of rich Parsi. During the 17th century, the centre of the Parsi community was transferred to the English factory in Surat. When Surat's importance declined in the beginning of the 18th century the Parsis began to move to Bombay. According to tradition the first Parsi, Dorabji Nanabhoy, settled in Bombay in 1640 while it was still in Portuguese hand. As early as 1773, the Parsis from Gujarat who had settled in Bombay were allotted a separate district in the centre of the town on the Malabar Hill.[11] About 3000 Parsis lived in Bombay in 1780, a decade later, fleeing from starvation, many more Parsis moved from Gujarat to Bombay.

According to J. Forbes, in the 70s and 80s of the 18th century, a considerable part of the land in Bombay belonged to Parsis, and also many beautiful houses, which they had either built themselves or bought from Englishmen who had gone home. Forbes, incidently notes the excellent knowledge of political affairs displayed by the Parsis and the absence of those castes prejudices which are characteristic of the Hindu and Muslim merchants.[12]

Muslim merchants in Gujarat at first were unable to benefit fully from the developing trade. But from the beginning of the 18th century onwards the link between the Muslim merchant and English became stronger. However these links between the two were never as close as those with the Parsis or Hindus. The Muslims continued to trade along the old established lines with the Middle East and East Africa. Two Gujarati castes, the Bohras and Khojas, occupied a dominant position among Muslim merchants.

The individuals who made Bombay their home during the year 1764-1780 were Amirchand Shah from Cambay, Megji Abhichand Shah from Radonpura, Krishna Narayan from Bessein, Rustom de Nadirshah, Framji Maneckji Karani Jamshedji Nanabhai Gazdar from Surat, Edulji Vacha from Navsari, Cawasji R. Narialwala from Hansot and Bhimji Dhanji Umarigar from Umara.[13] Together with the native merchants the private European traders too were engaged in commercial activities as Gazetteer records the names of John Petit and George Bowher as the best known interlopers on the Western coast who around 1680 started forming illicit trade relations with the Company's servants in India with a view to concentrate Company's trade into their own hands.[14] Thus, it follows that the European and native merchants of Bombay carried on a good deal of commerce totally in exclusion to the trade of East India Company. According to James Forbes the Bombay merchants secured pearls, raw silk, carmania wood, dates, dried fruits, rosewater, attar of roses and other commodities from Bussara, Muscat, Ormuz and the other parts in the Parsian Gulf while Arabia supplied them with coffee, gold, drugs and honey.[15] A number of ships annually freighted with cotton and bullion to China, returned laden with tea, sugar, porcelain, wrought silk, sankeens and a variety of useful ornamental articles from Java, Sumatra, Malasiya and the Eastern island. They brought spices, ambergris, perfumes, arrack and sugar, the cargoes from Madagascar, the Comoro Isles. Mozambique and other parts of the Eastern coast of Africa, consisted chiefly of ivory, slaves and drugs, while the different parts of India produced cotton, silk, muslin, pearls diamonds and every precious gems; together with ivory, sandalwood, pepper, carsia, cinnamon and other luxuries.[16] In 1770s, the demand for Indian cotton increased in China on account of famine that forced the Chinese to grow grains in place of cotton. When the demand for tea soared in Britain after 1784, the native and European both merchants of Bombay traded in tea which they brought from China in terms of paying them in raw cotton. However, it was the cotton, raw and later spun, in the final form of finished product that provided the foundation on which Bombay fortune rested in the nineteenth century.[17] Besides cotton it was also opium in which the native merchants of Bombay traded. The Jijibhais, the Camas and Dadyseth families all originally had opium interest.[18]

Thus, the great prospect of trade drew the attention of many other towards the island of Bombay and therefore the population of the island swelled considerably. Gillian Tindal estimates the population in 1780 as 1,13,726 which rose to 2,00,000 by 1806 and 2,40,000 by 1814.[19] This rise in population was due to the migration of men from the surrounding country with a view to trade or find work or escape famine. Whatsoever, the reason for this, it cannot be denied that the numbers, were generally on the increase. James Mckintosh also stated in 1804 that the monthly average of famine refugees relieved by Bombay government was 9,125,[20] due to which a large number of people arrived and population swelled in Bombay during this period. From 1803 onwards dwelling houses, godowns, shops and markets began to rise in Mandvi, Chakala and Omarkhadi section. By then the great prospect of trade made many to purchase land, build houses, and thus the foundation of one of the most prosperous of modern commercial classes was laid down.[21] Among these new settlers of the island were some six or eight families of Dasa Oswala Jain class who settled in Dongri street.[22] Many Parsis and several Mohammadans" notably the Memons who were described in a Persian Pamphlet of 1818 as fuel sellers, and the Khojas who were hawkers of parched rice."[23]

A most interesting census of population within fort wall in 1813 reveals the superiority of Parsi well established traders. According to it the population numbered 10,081 of which according to the official record 150 were English, 5,464 Parsis, 4061 Hindus, 775 Moors, 146 Portuguese and 105 Armanians.[24] It seems as if they were attracted towards the island by the great prospect of trade with China which had become the principal trading country in the turnover of Bombay's trade till 1805. The Banajis, Dadys Ready moneys were all China traders and together with that they also acted as brokers to the great European banking house and firms of the day. D.E. Wacha informs us that after 1814 the Memons and Khojas settled down in Bombay as traders because the life had become secure. Therefore, the population further swelled in numbers.[25] Of those who traded with China, Wacha names them as Gokuldas Tejpal, Jewraj Balloo, Motichand and some other Bania and Bhatia who traded in cotton and opium. Ramlal, a Marwari, was both a merchant and Philanthropist. Motichand the partner of Jamshedji Edulji Jijibhoy and Co. was another merchant. Rustomji Edulji Bottlewala carried on his opium business in Mopla building at Bora Bazar street.[26] Mr. Ebrahim Nooruddin was a Borah carrying trade with China. Together with them the English firms of Remington, Forbes, the Grahams, the Greys, the Peelcassel and a few others were very prominent.

Before 1813, the private trade could be carried on only with the licenses of the Company which had complete monopoly over eastern trade but after the passing of the Charter Act of 1813 the situation improved because the private persons were allowed to carry on trade as distinct from one another. William Milburn who himself was a trader has given the complete list of the European firms and native men who indulged in trade between 1803 and 1813. Among them 9 were Europeans, 4 Armanians, 14 Parsis, 4 Musalmans, 15 Hindu merchants and two Parsis as China agents.[27] There were some more Parsis in the year 1810 of Dadyseth family, Banaji Limjis, Jessi Jeevanji, Mencherji Jeevenji.[28] Among the Hindu merchants were Kessor Das Runsor Das, Vithal Das Keshow Ram, Madhav Das Ram Das, Shankar Sheth Babul Sheth, Dhakji Dadaji, Raghunath Dadaji, Tricum Das Lal Das, Ramchandra Shankar Shenoy, Naron Das Fulsli Das, Luckmichand Punjraj, Keshorji Shamji, Parasuram Bhowan, Virzlal Tulsi Das, Parmanand Raghunath Das, Soorsir Dumsir.[29] All these merchants were the residents of bombay who possessed great property and were the men of great integrity. Besides them there were some Borah merchants who carried on great trade with Gujarat and other places to northwards.

The defeat of the Peshwa in 1818 at the hands of English Company placed the later in more established way in Deccan. This led to the increase of trade in Bombay too. Consequently, by 1825 Bombay export started exceeding her import. By this time Bombay export was not confined to China only, it also increased with England. This increased trade led some European merchantile firms to found the 'Chamber of commerce' in 1836 which took an important share in the formation of public opinion in bombay.[30]

From the above mentioned data regarding, the big merchant houses in Bombay at the beginning of the 19th century one can very easily draw the conclusion that the native merchant houses were more than the European firms but in spite of their numerical strength, their commercial transactions were controlled by the British merchant capital which relied upon the political power and the greater concentration of its capital.

It is in fitness of things to now examine the activities of the merchants in Bombay during the 18th century. The Bombay merchants acted as junior partners of British merchant's capital and derived their profits by serving the foreigners. Thus, there existed a sort of cooperation between the British merchant firms and native merchants. At the beginning of the 18th century the East India Company conducted its trade in Bombay with the help of its official brokers who helped the Company in collection of taxes; they also worked as commercial agents. However, when the English Company came to have close relations with local merchants, these brokers became an obstacle hence the system of brokerage was abolished in 1737. Many Bombay traders were simply partners of British firms and as per the sources every European trading establishment had a Parsi partner, who usually provided most of the capital. How far the English firms valued the services of their Indian 'associate' can be understood from an incident in which a Parsi merchant Hormuz lost a huge sum of £ 2,00,000 as a result of speculation and then was helped by the firm of Charles Forbes with whom he had business relations.[31]

The Bombay traders were engaged in exporting goods, selling English manufactures in India and provisioning Bombay's population, garrison and fleet. In 1731, the East India Company presented a horse worth Rs. 500 to Landas, a Surat broker, as a mark of appreciation for his purchasing of all woolen goods, lead, copper and iron that had arrived from England.

The Bombay merchants were trading with the Middle-East. A. Hamilton met Indian Bania and Muslim merchants in the ports of the Persian Gulf early in the 18th century.[32] This trade which always showed a balance favorable to India, helped the English to cushion the constant foreign exchange deficit in their commerce with India. A petition sent by three Hindu merchants in 1741 to the authorities in Bombay is interesting in this connection. The merchants complained that the recent decision of Bombay Council abolishing the escort of warship for convoys sailing to the Arabian coast would seriously affect their old established commercial relations. Realizing that the

English administrators would not be moved by complaint about the cruel lot of their house-holds, but by commercial reasons the merchants continued. "By the loss of this beneficial trade from the north the Honourable Company would lose imports which contribute no trifling sum to customs. To your petitioners the failure of the north trade will be fatal, as it is mainly with this money and from the profits of this trade that we are able to carry on our business and maintain ourselves and families." The Company could not withstand such arguments and reversed its decision.[33]

Commerce with China carried on by Gujarat merchants was very important for the East India Company. Indian opium and cotton were the chief items exported to China. During the latter half of the 18th century large consignments of cotton were exported from Gujarat to Bengal and China. This commerce was in the hands of Bombay merchants both Englishmen and Guajaratis, who signed agreements with local traders whose job was to buy-up cotton in the villages. The fact that in 1801 seven merchants of Bombay purchased a quantity of cotton for export to China amounting to 850 thousand rupees already shows the size of these operations. Three of the merchants concerned in this deal were British and four Parsis *viz*. Hormud Borman, Peston Borman, Ardashir Dadiseth and Sokar Muncher Readymoney.[34]

At the beginning of the nineteenth century, commerce with China was the principal item in the turnover of Bombay. For example, in 1805 the export to China reached Rs. 64,73,600 while the export to Britain amounted only to Rs. 5,88,700.[35] But this does not mean that China trade was an end in itself. In fact, the export of cotton, and later of opium, to China was the principal source from which the East India Company obtained foreign currency enabling it to purchase Indian commodities to be sent overseas.

Maritime commerce with China and the other Asian countries contributed to the rise of Bombay shipping. The Parsis began to take interest in navigation in 1735. Ready money was the first Parsi to reach China in 1756. By 1792 the

Parsis owned more than twenty big ships mainly built in Bombay. Two of them had a displacement of more than 1000 tons. The biggest ship owners were the members of Wadia family, possessing six vessels, and members of Ready money family, who held three vessels. The richest ship owner in Bombay was also a Parsi, Rustomji Kovarjee Banajee. Members of the Davar family apparently the ancestors of Cowasji N. Davar, the first factory owners of Bombay[36] were also among the first ship owners of Bombay. During the second half of the 18th century and the beginning of the 19th century the principal source of the wealth of the merchants of Bombay was from shipping revenue.

These are some of the aspects of the collaboration between the Gujarati merchants and the British colonialists. Helping East India Company the Gujarati traders acquired considerable wealth. The Englishmen John Burnell, who visited India in 1711 wrote: "The Banias or merchants are not only rich and wealthy but like the rest of the world are covetous after more, placing the height of their happiness in riches, which they will scrap together by mean and petty officers, some of them amassing prodigious sums of money, being accounted worth 90 or 100 lakhs, or so many times a Rs. 1,00,000."[37] Evidence regarding the enormous riches accumulated by the Gujarati merchants co-operating with English is confirmed by documentary materials. For example in 1721, after the death of well known broker of Company the Parsi Rustom Manek, his heirs demanded the return of loan, amounting to Rs. 6,90,000 from the East India Company. After the Bombay Council of the Company refused to pay back the money, one of Maneck's sons obtained the agreement and the Chief Board of Directors reconsidered the matter. As a result, Maneck's heir received Rs. 5,64,000.[38]

Upto the end of the 18th century, the British energetically propogated handloom weaving in Bombay as in other factories throughout India.[39] By 1676, a regular industry had been established. The company imported silk and cotton and distributed it to the weavers who worked under a Mukadam and were paid partly in money and partly in rice.[40] The

Bombay Gazetteer quotes factual material on the handicrafts in Bombay during the 17th and 18th century. These documents permit us to form an opinion of the functions which the Indian middlemen so called Mukadam, performed. The Mukadam recruited weavers for the Company, supplied with them raw materials, granted them loans, collected the finished product and paid the weavers in money and foodstuffs. The trust that the Company placed in their agent was extremely great, for at times sums amounting to several thousand rupees passed through his hands for which he did not have to account, the agent was only obliged to handover a fixed quantity of manufactured goods.[41] Since the workers completely depended upon the Mukadam, he was able to exploit them in his own interest. Several Mukadams are mentioned by names in various documents. In the beginning of the 18th century, the Chief Master of the weavers working for the East India Company in Bombay was the Parsi Manna or manak.[42]

Handloom weaving in Bombay catered exclusively for the European market. The Company even sent weavers, dyers and other artisans to India in 1670 to show how the Indians manufactured those kinds of goods that were most likely to please the Europeans, and which could prove most profitable for the Company.

Thus, in the period when methods of primitive accumulation were applied in the colonial exploitation of India, the big Gujarati merchants in Bombay acted primarily as agents for British merchant's capital and received the greater parts of their profits for their services as brokers in regard to the overseas trade which was a British monopoly.

Upto the beginning of the 18th century the monopoly of foreign trade provided most of the profits for British capital carrying on primitive accumulation in Western India, while in Bengal and Bihar, conquered earlier by the British, pride of place belonged to tax robbery of the peasant (based on the fact that the colonial government assumed ownership of the land), direct exploitation of artisans by British merchant's capital and open military plunder of the population. During the latter half of the 18th century, the tragic fate of Bengal confirmed that merchant's capital, when it holds a position of dominance, stands everywhere for a system of robbery.[43] Bombay merchants were no exception to this corollary. Though they acquired huge amount of profit by way of working in co-operation with the British merchant capital, the later dominated the former's capital in all ways.

The close economic relations between the Indian merchants and money lenders and the East India Company created a favorable condition for the English to establish their political control. The Gujarati Banias gave military and political services to English as far back as the 17th century and took shelter in their fortified factories whenever there were dangers to them. Thus, Bombay which was a fortified castle became a safest refuge for them from the end of the 17th century. At the time, when the Marathas and English were at constant struggle with each other the Gujarati traders behaved as most loyal 'subjects' of the East India Company. They helped the British, with supplies and loans while they were fighting against the Marathas. The Gujarati Banias and Parsis served the colonial administration as councilors and agents. For example, two Parsi families of officials who had served the Peshwas for several generations took service with the English after the conquest of Maharashtra.[44] As the English Resident in Poona, Mountstuart Elphinston, highly valued the services of Kursheed Modi, a Parsi who had an excellent knowledge of local matters and served the British faithfully. It was this reason that he was poisoned by the Marathas.[45] Jawaharlal Nehru very aptly commented when he said that: "though the Indian merchant and manufacturing classes were rich and spread about all over country and even controlled the economic structure, they had no political power. Hence, there was no middle class strong enough or even consciously thinking of seizing power, as in some western countries."[46]

The Moneylenders

Before Bombay was taken over by the British the islands as well as the sea-board were inhabited by the Marathas. When

Bombay became the principal factory of the East India Company on the West Coast of India, as stated above many Gujaratis settled there, and during the 18th century they, perhaps, constituted the largest section of the inhabitants of Bombay. They carried on their trading business with the help of Marwari community which acted as middlemen in their whole sale trade.

The Marwari money lenders played an important part in the credit system of Bombay. The first reference to them is found in the Gazetteer of Bombay City which was published in 1909. Their penetration into Bombay must have taken place in connection with the powerful expansion of the money lending capital of Rajputana in Maharashtra, which began in the second quarter of the 19th century after the final defeat of the Peshwa government.

The classic description of the Marwari Bania's business activity in the Maratha village has been given in the Imperial Gazetteer of India which relates that the Bania from Marwar who wished to become a money lender usually brought his capital with him consisting of bills of exchange and gold and silver ornaments. After his arrival he met many members of his caste and other person whom he knew personally and from them got the helping hands in the form of credits. It is characteristic that the 'Capital' of the Marwari did not consist of money but either of valuables, which were to serve as security for loans, or of Bill of Exchange – Hundis – which circulated among the money lenders and local bankers who were working in close contact with each other.

The Marwari travelled around in the districts for a month or two studying the local conditions of trade. In the end, he settled down in the village which seemed to offer the best opportunities for profitable business operations. The Marwari rented a small house, opened a shop and began to trade in fabric, grain and groceries. He never miscalculated and never sold anything without making a profit. He showed great restraint in his personal expenditure. Within a short time, he was lending small sums of money taking as security household goods and ornaments. As soon as his connections expanded, the Marwari began to grant loan on the security of land or the future harvest. His stock of grain was growing every year. Some of the grains were sent to cities like Poona or Bombay and rest was kept as reserve to be used in case of bad harvest or a rise in price. Lending grain to peasants became one of the principal forms of the money lending activity of the Marwari and thus he enslaved the peasants.

The close connection between the commercial and money lending operations of the Marwaris was that the grain bought on the cheap rates from peasants was 'advanced' in usarious loans to same peasents. By applying pressure, the money lender squeezed grain out of the peasants for his wholesale operations too. The grain was sent to town where this trade was controlled by Marwari merchants. From commercial centers, the grain was taken to Bombay and other big cities.

The Marwaris were in the habit of granting usarious loans on the security of land, which led to the transfer of peasent holding into the hands of the money lenders, who got the peasents reduced to the status of being a tenant. According to Gazetteer of Bombay City and Island, the Gujarati or Marwari Bania, as a rule, permitted the debtor who had pledged his land to cultivate it as a tenant under the condition that he handed over from one half to three quarters of its product to the landlord. However it must be noted that communal ownership of land prevented the transfer of the land from the peasent debtor into the hands of the money lender.[47] The difficulties, that the peasents encountered when they had to pay their taxes and rents, were utilized by the money lender as a means of enslaving them. As per Buchanan, the money lenders and merchants frequently advanced money to peasents to pay their rents, and afterwards contended to take one half of the crop for the advance and for interest. These advances were sometimes made six month before the crop was reaped.[48] The above mentioned two example of Madras Presidency are sufficient enough to establish that the modus-operandi of merchants and money lenders in Maharashtra was no better than there.

As a result of tax collecting in which the Marwari trading and money lending caste engaged members of these castes frequently occupied high positions in the state machinery too. It is well known that the ancestors of the Marwari capitalist, Gopaldas Mohta, many times headed the administrative apparatus of Bikaner and was granted Jagirs and various privileges for their military and administrative services.[49]

Tax farming also helped many members of the trading and money lending caste to advance to high posts in the administration of the Mughal state. Todarmal a member of Agarwal, a Marwari caste, organized and headed the financial department of Akbar at the end of the 16th century. A Jain, Kharsukhrai, was treasurer of the Mughals and responsible for paying the troops. His successor P. D. Ramchandar was in-charge of remitting revenue payments to Delhi.[50] In the beginning of 18th century; the Gujarati Shroff (banker) Anandrai Mashraf was minister of the last Mughal Viceroy in Gujarat.

Provisioning of the troops and the resale of plunder amassed during the campaign were the most important services rendered by the money lenders of the feudal class. A banker in Mughal India grew rich if he received the office of the 'Modi' *i.e.* that of a supplier of provisions to the army.[51] The bankers, purveyors had agents in various centers of the country along the roads used by the army, whose job was to supply the army on move. The well-known French traveler J. B. T. Travernier, who visited India towards the end of the 17th century, wrote: "A great part of the money belonging to state is always in the hands of the Shroffs who derive from it considerable profits. According to the rules of the country, the troops are paid monthly, but the majority of soldiers as well as many captains and other officers do not wait till the end of the month but borrow money from the Shroffs who take 18-20 percent interest per annum.[52]

The Marathas employed a similar system to finance and provision the army on the march. Predatory raids were for the Maratha states one of the principal source of revenue but the organization of such a raid depended on whether a local bankers was prepared to advance the money necessary for the maintenance of the army. In 1760 when Marathas marched to north for the decisive fight against Afgans, the Peshwa Balaji Bajirao was able to give only 200 thousand rupees in cash to Sadashivrao Bhau, the commander of the army, while the expense of the campaign exceeded 500-600 thousand rupees per month.[53] One of the chief functions of the big moneylenders and bankers charged with supplying the Maratha troops during campaign was to advance money to the so called Banjaras with which the later were to purchase grain and bring it to camp. Accounts of British eyewitness confirm that big moneylenders helped in supplying provision to the Maratha troops.

The bankers were instrumental in plundering by means of taxing the regions seized by the Maratha feudal, for whom the phrases 'to wage war' and to 'collect taxes' were synonymous.[54] It was seldom possible to collect, the taxes in cash. The Marathas, therefore, sought the help of the local banker who gave them a bill of exchange. The local authorities undertook to repay with interest the sum for which the bill was drawn. The conqueror could present the bill for payment in any part of India.[55] The highly developed system of Bill of exchange was thus used by the Marathas during their forays to obtain the greatest possible amount of tribute in the shortest time. This could be possible because the corresponding bankers as members of the same caste maintained close relations with each other. Dr. D. R. Gadgil observes regarding the use of bills of exchange and the function of the bankers to remit revenue payments. "Banking houses might be authorized to receive payments made either by local officials or functionaries and remit them to headquarters. Even where they were not so directly authorized, exchange business would arise out of the needs of remittance."[56]

The supply of luxury articles, weapons, horses and other imported goods to the nobility was final form in which the trading and money lending caste served the feudal. Trade in these goods helped to spread the business connections of the

Indian merchants far beyond the borders of the country. Thus, Indian merchants played an active role in the trade during the 17th and 18th century.

Money lending was an important source of revenue for the mercantile and money lending castes. "Coining was not highly centralized and there were large numbers of local mints. The variety of coins put into circulation was thus large. Moreover, coins were liable to deteriorate and new issues of even the same, mint were usually at a premium. Large transactions, therefore, involved operations with a variety of coins and fixing of their mutual values in exchange. This led to creation of agencies ready to accept payment in a variety of coins or ready to exchange one type of coinage into another. Sometimes, the money changers were specialized as such, but usually money-changing was combined with other financial or banking business."[57] The fact that coins minted from the variety of mints circulated in the country provided the Shroffs with many opportunities to enrich themselves by changing coins and assessing their value in terms of the leading currency. According to Travernier, the Shroff would, after having evaluated a certain quantity of coins sew them up in bags, indicate their value on it and affix his personal seal. When the bag passed from hand to hand, the Shroff confirmed the value of its contents and received his fixed interest.[58]

Because commercial and financial operations were conducted on an enormous scale, both according to their volume and the territory they covered, the Indian merchants and bankers had to create a complicated and at the same time reliable credit and information system. This system was based on caste organization. Pt. Jawaharlal Nehru remarked that "The India's Banking system was efficient and well organized throughout the country and the Hundis or bills of exchange issued by great business or financial houses were honored everywhere in India, as well as in Iran, and Kabul and Herat, and Tashkent and other places in central India. There was an elaborate network of agents, jobbers, brokers and middlemen... a very rapid and indegenous system of communicating news and market prices had been evolved."[59]

The methods used in commerce and monetary operations were handed down from generation to generation and further developed by each of them. It had produced excellent business abilities among the members of trading and money lending castes and their capital became influencial particularly in the early days of the 18th century.

Trading and money lending in Maharashtra developed on similar line. Upto the 18th century, Maharashtra was a backward region. The towns were not so much independent centers of commerce and handicraft. In the 18th century, the formation of a federation of Maratha feudal states centered on Maharashtra and the rapid development of feudal relations created new conditions for urban life.[60] The vast amount of riches that the Marathas amassed by robbing the conquered regions and the intensified exploitation of the local peasentry, caused an increased flow of orders from the local feudal chiefs and the feudal states, which spent enormous sums on the maintenance of army, administration and court. It should be stressed that the means available to pay the artisans consisted of the rent tax and war booty *i.e.* the demand had a natural basis and greatly depended on the prosperity of the feudal state. The artisan's dependence on state orders was reflected in the fact that to a certain extent the state regulated the handicraft industries by means of an ordering system and by granting individual the monopoly of manufacturing a given order. The consolidation of the feudal Maratha state and the extension of its territorial limits far beyond Maharashtra proper created extremely favorable conditions for the activity of big merchant capital. Such transactions as collecting and remitting the rant tax, buying-up war booty, granting loans to the feudal lords and supplying goods to them and to the army, and the growth of maritime commerce provided traders and money lenders with many opportunities to enrich themselves.

Money changing and determining the value of coins were important sources of profit for bankers and money lenders in feudal Maharashtra. According to R. D. Choksey, "There was, under the late government so large a number of siccas... that the Shroffs Sawkars and merchants defrauded the public at will. Bankers often resorted to forging and counterfeiting money."[61]

But the principal source of profit for money lenders was the collection of rent tax. Usually the peasants gave a promissory note to the money lender who paid his fallen dues to the head of the village community. When the later had to remit the tax to the higher officials of the state, he in turn, gave a promissory note to a bigger money lender who then paid the tax in cash. This mode of payment was most prevalent, so much so that it is estimated that scarcely 25 percent of the revenue was paid directly in money.[62] The rapid expansion of commercial and financial activities caused an immigration of merchants and bankers from adjoining regions of Maharashtra. As a result the majority of big local merchants and tax farmers in the state were Brahmins, [63] while the leading positions in large scale commerce and banking continued to be occupied by Gujarati and Marwari Banias who had begun to immigrate into Maharashtra. Consequently, the whole of the Maharashtra came to be divided by both into their specific sphere of influence. The Gujaratis dominated in the Western part while Marwaris dominated the Eastern part of Maharashtra by the time of early 18th century and started operating their capital in two ways. Firstly, lending money to extravagant members of the upper classes, particularly land-owners. Secondly, by lending money to small producers who possessed their own conditions of labour which included the artisans.[64] Thus, although the trading and money lending capital got accumulated to the best extent but it could not be used for industrial productions on account of the fear from the side of state to the big money lender or merchant. The state had the tendency to get hold of the wealth accumulated by the merchants and the money lenders even by using the most savage tortures. This was perhaps, the reason why the money lenders kept hidden their capital in form of money, bills of exchange and precious stones rather than land, building or enterprises which could be seen by the state and thus could invite trouble to them.

Speculalation Business

Apart from money lending business, the mercantile and moneyed classes in the city performed an enormous amount of speculative business on behalf of up-country constituents, residents in all parts of India, acting in fact as commission agents for the later. Bonafied nature of this business was performed in government promissory notes by private merchants and brokers, in the shares of joint stock companies by the same classes, in cotton, in seeds such as linseed, rapeseed, castor seed, poppy seed, cotton seed, ginger, in wheat, Rangoon rice, in Calcutta made gunny bags, and in gold and silver. The Gazetteer of Bombay City and Island (1909) records that the speculation took place at Wadi Bunder and Pydhoni while in silver it was carried on in Chandi Bazar (Shaikh Memon Street) and in case of stocks and share in Dalal Street at Fort.[65] A certain amount of speculation in opium also took place.

The aforesaid Gazetteer also records a judgement of late Sir Charles Farran in 1892 in the case of J. H. Jod Vs Lakhamdas that "It appears to be the practice in Bombay to enter largely into contracts for the purchase and sale of produce still ungrown for future delivery. The vicissitudes of the market frequently rendered rebate advisable and a highly speculative mode of business is thus engineerd. The expected produce is sold and resold over and over again. Sanguine minds engage in these transactions hoping for profit and trusting to their own forecasts, as to the probable future of the market."[66]

The above judgement bears testimony to the fact that speculative business had become a future of commercial life in Bombay and was called as Satta. "This business involved the making of the contracts for the sale or purchase of any commodity or produce or manufactured article or stocks and shares at a specified rate deliverable at specified future time, the seller or buyer, as the case may be, trusting to his own calculation or forecast of the market rate on such specified date. The transaction was as a rule not followed by actual delivery of goods, so that the business done is often entirely disproportionate to the actual quantity of goods available in the market on the due date, and the transaction degenerated into simple gambling on the differences in rates. However, wherever the parties were desirous of bringing the contracts to its logical conclusion the actual delivery and acceptance did take place. In order to sustain such cases in the law courts, in many cases, the persons involved in such business did enter into duly signed and stamped agreements."[67]

Thus, a good deal of speculative business was done in Bombay by the local commission agents on behalf of up-country constituents. As per the English law a commission agent was not allowed to have same contracts with many constituents at one time but in practice the Bombay speculative merchants could enter into amalgamated contracts provided if they did not change the rates of the substituted contract other than contained in the original agreement.[68] Due to such practices, the up-country constituents did not suffer because they obtained what they required on the due date. But if any one of the substituted parties failed to fulfill his contract or became insolvent, then the loss fell upon the commission agent. Another speculative practice was that of making of forward contracts of sale by endorsement and tendering to purchaser of delivery orders issued by persons other than the persons who contracted to sell but in this practice no reference was made to the quantity of goods actually available. These orders passed through many hands before they reached the parties who were prepared to take delivery of the goods specified in the orders. The intermediate parties stood thus in a definite relation to one another. Each of them was a purchaser from the party who gave him the order and was a seller to the party to whom he in turn endorsed it. His seller having performed the sale contact with him and he in his turn having performed his contract with his vendee. In this way, any number of parties could perform a series of contracts in respect of one set of goods. A check upon the free transfer of delivery orders from hand to hand in the case of forward-contracts had been devised and consisted in the insertion of a provision binding the buyer alone to take delivery. But the provision was unpopular, as it favored the seller at the expense of the buyer. The rate of commission charged by agents for speculative business in gold and silver varied from one to 4 annas percent, in cotton-seeds and wheat from 4 to 12 annas or one rupee percent, on the value of the goods sold or purchased.[69]

In the Marwari Bazar in Bombay, gambling in differences came to be termed as Teji Mundi contracts which meant normal contract for the sale or purchase of specified goods at specified future dates on the basis of the market price as on those date to the wager the contracts were divided into three classes [70] *viz* :

(*a*) Teji contracts of nominal contracts under which the decision of the wager rested upon the rise of the market at the specified future date.

(*b*) Mundi contracts under which the decision of the wager rested upon the fall or the market at the specified future.

(*c*) Teji Mundi contracts under which the giver of the stake and proposer of the bet and the option of declaring certain number of days before the specified date whether he would nominally buy from or sell to the other party. In the former case, the rise of the market and in the later the fall of the market determined the wager.

Thus, the relation between the two parties in this was not that of buyer and seller but that of proposer and acceptor of bet. The stake was deposited either in cash or in the form of Hundi falling due on the date specified for performance of the nominal contract, that is to say the date on which the ruling market price was to be taken as meaning who had won the bet. Another form of gambling in differences, which some merchants regarded as a genuine form of business was Gali-Satta,[71] or forward contracts giving the purchaser the option of declaring five or more days before the due date whether he will take delivery or only pay differences at specified rates. The gambling in opium was known as Ank Satta.[72] in which the wager was determined by the receipt of the evening telegram from Calcutta. In the case of speculation in promissory notes and shares, the agreements between the parties were usually in writing and were duly stamped.

The above said Gazetteer also referes to the rain-gambling in Bombay during monsoon days. It was done in Pydhoni[73] where a house used to be rented at high price for four months of the monsoon by some twenty or more native capitalists. This was known as Barsaat-Ka-Satta and was divided into two forms known as Calcutta Mori and Lakadi Satta. In the former case, wagers were laid as to whether the rain would filter in a certain fixed time through a specially prepared box filled with sand, the banker settling the rates or prices of the wager by the appearance and direction of the clouds while in the second case, the winning or losing of the wager depended upon whether the rainfall within a certain period was sufficient to fill the gutter of a roof and overflow. The name Lakadi Satta was due to the fact that a piece of wood was fixed to spout to help the accumulation of water. The time for this type of Satta was between 6 to 9 a.m., 9 a.m. to 12 noon and 6 p.m. to 12 mid-night and the rates varied according to the signs of rain in the heavens and the amount of time left before the period within which bets could be booked or expired. This practice was put down by government after which the other speculative practices gained more momentum.

Thus, from the above accounts it follows that the Gujarati and Marwari Banias were engaged in the money lending and trading business in Maharashtra even since the days of the Mughal's rule and Portuguese rule in the city of Bombay. They might have made the island as their area of operation, after it was acquired by the British, because of the security that was provided to the native immigrants as per the policy of East India Company. By collaborating with the English firms both communities appear to have accumulated a good amount of capital that they further invested into the capitalist enterprises in the 19th century. However, a point to be noted in this connections is that it was mainly the Gujarati and Parsi Banias who availed the new opportunities given to them through their collaboration with English capital and they began with the capitalist enterprises but the Marwari community remained behind because they did not lose their connection with their original homeland. They remained engaged in widespread financial and money lending transaction only. The fact is that the commercial operations of the Marwari local bankers and merchant were directed towards Rajputana and central India. Otherwise, they occupied prominent positions as brokers in the wholesale trade of the town. Among the indigenous bankers, who came from the native states and settled down in Bombay were no doubt the Marwari bankers whose aggregate capital according to Digby amounted to Rs. 60 million.[74] However, this community did not play any significant role in the Textile Mill Industry of Bombay as their names in any case do not appear either among the managing agents or the Directors of Bombay factories. In fact, very little is known about the scale and nature of the Marwari's businesses activities in Bombay even by the close of the 19th century.

However, the account of money lending and trade would be incomplete if the reference to a Hindu Shroff and businessman, Rama Kamathi, is not made. His ancestors came from Goa to Bombay during the days of Portuguese but Rama Kamathi rose to fame in 1680. He started his carrier as a simple Shroff and rose to become a wealthy and important businessman of 18th century Bombay, with an income of over Rs. 37,000/- per year. However, he became the victim of his misfortune and was imprisoned though wrongly, by the English on the ground of having betrayed the English trust by joining in a conspiracy with Kanhoji Angre. His property worth more than Rs. 60,000/- was confiscated and his family was left in poverty. Rama Kamathi himself died as a broken man. As seen above, mercantile money lending and speculate activities also led to growth of capitalism in Bombay.

REFERENCES

1. William Milburn: *Oriental Commerce of Principal Places in the East Indies, China and Japan*, Vol. I, p. 171, (Black Party and Co., 1813), p. 294.
2. J. D. G. D. Cunha: *'Origin of Bombay'*, pp. 294-295.

3. *Material towards statistical account of the Town and Island of Bombay*, pt-(Hist.)

   (Bombay Gazetteer XXV Bombay, 1893)-64.
4. J. D G. D. Cunha: *op.cit.*, p. 295.
5. G. B. C.I., Vol. I, p. 168.
6. *Ibid*, p. 168.
7. J. Fryer: *A New Account of East India and Persia*, Vol. I, p. 239.
8. Jawaharlal Nehru: *'Discovery of India'*, p. 310.
9. C.H. Rao: *Indian Biographical Dictionary* (Madras, 1950), p. 325.
10. D. R. Gadgil: *Origins of the Modern Indian Business Class – An Interim Report*, p. 20.
11. Ch. Fawcett: *'English Factories in India' (Oxford 1936),??* Vol. I, p. 79.
12. J. Forbes: *Oriental Memoirs* – D, pp. 385-386.
13. S.M. Edwardes: *The Rise of Bombay*, p. 207.
14. *G.B.C.I.*, Vol. I, p. 75.
15. James Forbes: *'Oriental Memoirs' quoted by Gillian Tindal in 'City of Gold'*, p. 134.
16. *Ibid.*, p. 134.
17. *Ibid.*, pp. 134-35.
18. *Ibid.*
19. *Ibid.*, p. 168.
20. *G.B.C.I.*, Vol. I, p. 160.
21. S.M. Edwardes: *op.cit.*, p. 236.
22. *Ibid.*
23. G.B.C.I., Vol. I, p. 160.
24. D. E. Wacha: *'Shells from the Sands of ...,'* p. 4.
25. *Ibid.*, p. 416.
26. *Ibid.*, p. 427.
27. William Milburn: *op.cit.*, Vol. I, p. 234.
28. S. M. Edwards: *op.cit.*, Vol. I, p. 234.
29. Milburn: *Op.cit.*, Vol. I., p. 234.

30. G.B.C.I., Vol. I, p. 142.

31. *Handbook for India (Bombay-1857), Pt.-2, 283.*

32. A. Hamilton: *A New Account of the East Indies,* 1-41-91.

33. *Ibid., I, 274.*

34. J. Douglas: *Bombay and Western India (London, 1893),* I, pp. 241-242.

35. J.M. Maclean: *A Guide to Bombay, Historical, Statistical, and Descriptive (Bombay-1880),* p. 105.

36. W. H. Coates: *The Old Country Trade (London, 1911),* pp. 51-90.

37. J. Burnell: *Bombay in the Days of Queen Anne (London 1933),* p. 110.

38. *Gujarat Population, Hindus (Bombay Gazetteer, IX, PT-Bombay 1899),* p. 196.

39. *Indian Textile Journal, July 1924.*

40. *G. B. C. I., (Bombay 1909),* Vol. I, p. 462.

41. *Trade and Fortifications, Bombay Gazetteer, XXVI, Pt-2 (Bombay, 1894),* pp. 131, 132.

42. C.H. Fawcett: *English Factories in India, (Oxford, 1936),* I. p. 57.

43. Karl Marx: *Capital,* Vol. III, p. 325.

44. *Minutes of Evidence taken before Select Committee on the Government of Indian Territories, (London, 1835),* p. 294, in V. I. Pavlov: *The Indian Capitalist Class (New Delhi, 1999),* p. 90.

45. *English record of Maratha History, Poona residency correspondence, XII-Pt, I, 1811-1815 (Bombay, 1950),* pp. 323, 324.

46. Jawaharlal Nehru: *Discovery of India,* pp. 32, 263.

47. A. Sarda Raju: *Economic Conditions in the Madras Presidency, 1800-1850 (Madras, 1941),* p. 134.

48. F. Buchanan: *A Journey from Madras, (London, 1804),* Vol. I, p. 265.

49. *The Rajputana Gazetteer (Simla, 1880)-III, 27, Indian Year Book, 1947 (Calcutta, 1947), 1449.*

50. B. Bhargava: *Indigenous Banking in Ancient and Medieval India (Bombay – 1934),* pp. 29-32.

51. *Ibid.,* p. 29.

52. Quoted by V. I. Pavlov: *in Indian Capitalist Class (New Delhi, 1999),* p. 42.

53. *Ibid.*, p. 43.
54. J. Forbes: *op.cit.*, II, p. 50.
55. *Ibid.*
56. D. R. Gadgil: *op.cit.*, p. 32
57. *Ibid.*
58. V.I. Pavlov: *op.cit.*, p. 46.
59. Jawaharlal Nehru: *op.cit.*, p. 262.
60. Gadgil: *op.cit.*, p. 15.
61. R. D. Chokesy: *Economic History of Bombay, Deccan and Karnataka: 1818-1868. (Poona, 1945)*, p. 53.
62. *Ibid.*, p. 84-85.
63. Gadgil: *op.cit.*, p. 15.
64. Karl Marx: *Capital (Moscow 1959) III*, p. 581. *(Characteristics Preceding Capitalist Production).*
65. *G. B. C. I. (Bombay, 1909)* Vol. I., p. 300.
66. *Ibid. (Quotation taken by Gazetteer from 'Indian Law Reports', Bombay series, XVI)*, p. 299.
67. *Ibid.*, p. 299.
68. *Ibid.*, p. 300.
69. *Ibid.*, p. 301.
70. *Ibid.*
71. *Ibid.*, p. 302.
72. *Ibid.*
73. V. I. Pavlov: *op.cit.*, p. 259.
74. *Ibid.*

4

Commercial, Trading and Moneylending Capitalists (1801-1850 A.D.)

Bombay became the centre of main trade route of foreign trade during the first half of the 19th century which further extended far into the interior. The Bombay's foreign trade began rapidly increasing after the conquest of Maharashtra in 1818.[1] By the middle of the 19th century, more than a third of India's overseas trade passed through the port of Bombay. The growing flow of British commodities encouraged an even greater number of Gujarati merchants of all types, from a big wholesale dealer to the small shopkeeper, to act as middlemen. Describing the Bohra merchants from Gujarat who traded in central India J. Malcolm writes: "The Bohras, who came from the sea-coast of Gujarat into Central India, have imported the improvement of European settlements, even in the construction of their houses and furniture: They are the chief medium through which the trade in European articles is carried on."[2] An English traveler Maria Graham, who visited India in 1809 wrote about the Bania merchants of Gujarat that "In Bombay, there are a good many Banyas or travelling merchants, who came mostly from Gujarat and Roam about the country with muslins, cotton cloth, and shawls to sell. On opening one of their bales, I was surprised to find at least of its contents of British manufacture and such articles were much cheaper than those of equal fineness from Bengal and Madras excepting a particular kind of Chintz made at Poonah, and painted with gold and silver, there are no fine cotton cloths made on this side of the Peninsula."

Maria Graham's further account makes it clear that the British fabrics, she saw in the sale of the Gujarati traders, were machine made. She goes on to say how strange it seemed that cotton exported to England worked up there and returned as cloth to India, should sell here at a lower price than the local manufacturers, where labour was so cheap. She believed that this was due to the unsettled state of affairs and the difficulty of sending goods to different parts of the country, but the chief reason seemed to be the fact that England employed machinery.[3]

In the period of the exploitation of India by industrial capital, the British capitalists did not merely confine themselves to selling their factory produced commodities in India but also exported raw materials (cotton, jute, indigo) and foodstuffs from India. Indian merchants, especially, those from Gujarat collaborated with the colonial regime made enormous fortunes by trading in opium, and began to take part in the cotton export. In the twenties of the last century, the Gujarati compradors headed by Jeejeebhoy, the richest merchant, started with the backing of Maratha traders to export cotton from Maharashtra. Cotton export from Gujarat began even earlier. Cotton export trade in Western India was almost entirely in the hands of Gujarati merchants upto the middle of the 19th century.[4] J. Chapman, an English economist, who studied the Indian cotton trade explained that the British trader's poor knowledge of the North-Western parts of India, the absence of a network of agents and the competition of the natives, accounted for the weak representation of British merchant's capital in these regions.[5] The real reason however was, undoubtedly, that the Marathas withstood the conquerors for so long a time.

J. Chapman, who was an English eye-witness too, has written the following account of the organization of the cotton trade in 1836: "The exporters of cotton to the coast are chiefly opulent individuals and native firms of Bombay. They have Gomashtas, agents or factors who have located themselves at Khamgaum (a cotton growing centre in Maharashtra) from whence they send out subordinates to the several Pergunnatis, to make advances to Patel's (village headman) and substantial ryots of village about two months previous to the gathering, at 2 percent per month. Such security is taken as can be got and they deem good, usually of Mahajuns (money lenders) or able and wealthy Patel's themselves. They likewise purchase cotton from the Mahajuns who are settled in Kasbas, and almost every respectable village in the country, these Mahajuns having made advances to the ryots in the similar way. When the cotton begins to come in, the Principal Talookdars and Mahajuns of large towns and points meet and fix what is called a Sahookar's price and receive the wool from the producers (cleared from the seed) at the Kasba or the village itself. They take a discount of one rupee per nug on account of the advances made by them."[6]

The penetration of commodity relations into the Indian village caused trading and money lending capital to expand its sphere of activities. This occurred first of all in the parts of the country which started producing industrial raw materials. But in the first half of the 19th century, barter was still used as a means of extracting raw material even in Gujarat, a relatively advanced region. In order to obtain a small quantity of oil needed for lighting, the peasent who had no ready money gave the local shopkeeper cotton or grain in exchange which the later sold in town.[7] Although the shopkeeper made use of every opportunity to enslave the peasent, such as the debt which the peasent incurred in the shop, the loss of his cattle, failure of crops, a wedding, and in the final resort he simply fell back on cheating and swindling his illiterate customer.[8] The self-sufficiency of the peasent household permitted the agriculturists to retain a certain independence in relation to the trading and money lending capital.

Only gradual increase of elements of commodity production in the peasent household brought about a situation where the peasent was more and more frequently forced to borrow money from the userer, not as a consumer who cannot satisfy his personal requirements by means of his own natural economy, but as a small commodity producer who has to turn to money lender mainly because his economy depended on the market. In both cases, the loans-apart from rare exceptions, were of course intended for purpose of consumption and were not made with the intention of investing the money in production. This apparent similarity was due to the fact that the object of both the natural economy of the peasent and small commodity producing peasent economy in colonial India remained personal consumption, not accumulation in order to expand production. Not until the sixties of the 19th century can one observe the phenomenon in India that the peasents' dependence on money lender increased when there was a good harvest of industrial corps and their prices fell and, on the contrary, the dependence of the peasent somewhat decreased when poor harvests caused the prices of agricultural products to rise. Finally, it is only from this time onwards that the conditions prevailing in the capitalist world market began to exert a determining influence on the output of the Indian peasent economy, by way of the Indian trading and money lending capital.

The agriculturists' dependence on the trader had already increased in the twenties and thirties of the 19th century when the peasent households turned to the cultivation of export crops. The Gujarati peasents increasingly depended for their supply of grain on merchants, who grew rich on this trade, especially at times when the harvests were bad. The population in the Northern Provinces of West India always suffered from great famines. The Bania merchants who possessed big stores of grain refused to sell them during the first famine year, in the hope that later they would make enormous profits.[9] The feudal exploitation of the peasents and their exploitation by taxation went together with their enslavement by the money lender. As has already been seen, a whole network of middlemen and agents consisting of landlords, urban money lenders, the top strata of the countryside, and the village money lenders were employed by the Gujarati compradors to exploit the peasents. The enslaved peasents were forced to sell their cotton at a reduced price. The Indian landlords and merchants, thus, enabled British industrial capital to obtain the raw material for the British cotton industry at a cheaper rate.

The dependence of the East India Company on the services of Gujarati merchants compelled it to admit them to the trade with China, an exclusive monopoly which the Company jealously guarded against all European traders. The merchants of Bombay sold opium and cotton to China and brought from there tea and other commodities which for the most part were re-exported to Europe.

The Indian production of opium was concentrated in the Eastern part of the country, in the Banaras and Patna areas and in Central India, in the Malwa region, from where it was sent via Bombay to Canton. Although opium was produced around Banaras and Patna, the merchants of East India were unable to derive much benefit from the traffic on opium nor the East India Company completely monopolized this trade from 1799 to 1803.

The merchants of Bombay who collaborated with colonialists were in a more favorable position since the bulk of the marketable opium passed through their hands. It would, however, be wrong to assume that the British colonialists did not control the opium trade in western India. After the final defeat of the Maratha state in 1818, the production of opium was declared to be the exclusive privilege of the Princess of Indore and Gwalior and of other native rulers. But the buying up of opium was the monopoly of the East India Company. It brought opium to Bombay and sold it by auction to local merchants. In 1831, the British cancelled their agreement with the Princes, and abolished the monopoly which Malwa had in regard to the production of opium, at the same time handing over the marketing of opium to private traders. But the British imposed extremely high transit duties on the opium exported through the port of Bombay.[10]

The opium trade was carried on directly by the merchants

of Gujarat. One of them Hathi Singh, who was a member of the Nagarseths, an old family of banker from Ahmadabad, regularly sent large consignments of opium, containing upto thousand chests to China.[11]

The opium export began from Bombay port as early as 1670 but it could become an important item of trade only in 1713 when the British East India Company found the trade in opium immensely profitable. It started exporting opium to China on which the Chinese government put ban in 1729 after which the British East India Company resorted to dubious methods of opium importation to China by licensing the private traders, generally Parsis in Bombay, to carry on export of opium to China illegally, by smuggling.[12] This became a very profitable trade and many Parsi, Konkani, Gujarati, Hindus and some English firms in Bombay indulged in traffic in opium and amassed huge wealth.[13] The early 19th century generation of the Bombay cotton mill owners of the latter half of the 19th century made fortune by traffic in opium. William Millburn who himself was a trader, has given the complete list of the European firm and native men who indulged in trade between 1803 and 1813,[14] In fact, there were more Parsis in the year 1810 of whom history makes no mention. They were Bomanji Byramji of Dadyseth family, Banaji Limjis, Jessi Jivanji, Mancherji Jivanji.[15] Among the Hindu merchants were Kessor Das Runsor Das, Vithal Das Keshav Ram, Madhav Das Ram Das, Shankar Sheth Babul Sheth, Dhakji Dadaji, Raghonath Dadaji, Tricum Das Lal Das, Ramchandra Shankar Shenoy, Naron Das Tulsi Das, Luckmichand Punjraj, Keshawaji Shamji, Parasuram Bhowan, Virzlal Tulsidas, Parmanand Raghunath Das, Soorsir Dumasir.[16] All these merchants were the residents of Bombay who possessed great properties and were the men of great integrity. Besides them, there were some Borah merchants who carried on great trade with Gujarat and other places to northward. As has already been stated earlier that the volume of trade increased much after the conquest of Maharashtra by the English as a result of which Bombay export started exceeding her import on account of China trade hence some European mercantile firms took up the lead to found the

Chamber of Commerce in 1836 with which the native merchant Dadabhoy Pestonji was also associated.

D. E. Wacha also informs us that after 1814 the Memons, Khojas settled down in Bombay as traders.[17] Of those who traded with China, D. E. Wacha names Gokul Das Tejpal, Jivraj Balloo, and some other Bania and Bhatia traders in cotton and opium. Ramlal, a Marwari, was both a merchant and philanthropist. Motichand, the partner of Jamshedji Jeejeebhoy and Co., was another merchant. Rustomji Edulji Bottlewala carried on his opium business in Mopla building at Borah Bazar Street.[18] Mr. Ebrahim Nooruddin was a Bohra carrying trade with China. Together with them, the English firm of Remington, Forbes, the Grahams, the Greys, the Peelcassel and others were most prominent.

The acknowledged king of the merchants of Bombay was Jamshedji Jijibhoy. In the first three decades of the 19th century, through his activities in the opium trade, he managed to amass enormous fortune amounting to thirty million rupees, which he deposited in the British bank of Bombay. [19] Postans who visited Bombay in 1838, called him the wealthiest Parsi of Bombay.[20] Jamshedji Jijibhoy was born in 1783, in a family of modest means. At the age of 12, he was apprenticed in the shop of his uncle, a glass merchant. But Jijibhoy did not remain for long in his uncle's shop. His biographer Jhabvala wrote that opium, silk and similar expensive goods opened enormous prospect to the enterprising young man. Jijibhoy soon went to China, where he traded in cotton. But he was unsuccessful and returned poor in a pitiful state. However the failure did not discourage him and he made three more journeys to China for filling up his purse. Even the French navy, which operated along the shipping routes, once seized a vassal with a cargo belonging to Jijibhoy, did not stop him. He was connected with one of the leading English firms in Bombay, Crawford and Company. In 1824, he headed a group of Bombay Merchants, who began to export cotton from Berar.[21] Sir, Jamshedji Jijibhoy had also invested in shipbuilding industry and was the biggest dock-owner employing on the average approximately 3000 workers.[22]

Many other merchants of Gujarat, the forefathers of the richest industrialists of Bombay and Ahmadabad, made their fortune by trading in opium. Opium Trade caused a revival of selling activities in Bombay during the first half of the 19th century. By 1840, *i.e.* the time of the Opium War waged by British in China, the greater part of opium traffic was in the hands of the Parsis. Dadabhoy Rustomji alone lost, according to British estimate, upto two million rupees when opium was confiscated by the Chinese authorities.[23] Special clippers were built in Calcutta for the illicit traffic in opium. One of these ships, which belonged to Parsi Rustomji Kawasji, could make the journey from Calcutta to Macao in sixteen days. It is no mere co-incidence that during the war with China the Parsi opium merchants placed their vassal at the disposal of British commands to be used as troop carriers. The ships of the Parsis were the principal means of transport which enabled the British to convoy their soldiers to the Chinese ports. Rustomji Kawasji alone supplied fourteen boats for this purpose.[24] The smuggling of opium to China continued till agitation started in England against opium trade and House of Commons passed a resolution against traffic in opium in 1895 against smuggling of opium to China. This trade, however, continued, though in smaller volume, even upto the eve of the opening of the second decade of 20th century when it became insignificant, by 1917.[25]

The Wadias were the biggest ship-owners in Bombay during the first half of the 19th century. Between 1786 and 1842, they owned sixteen large vessels. Ready money had seven, Kama had seven, Patel had eight and so on. After the British-Chinese war, however, many of the Parsi shipping companies disappeared. This war partly because of the fact China started producing and selling its own opium and partly to the development of steam navigation. In 1845, the Bombay Steam Navigation Company, a firm, with a capital of one million rupees was formed, which owned one steamship making trips to Ceylone and Karachi. The management of the Company consisted of English men and native merchants from Bombay. But the large shipping companies that were later set up in

Bombay were purely British, with the exception of short lived companies founded during the cotton boom.[26] Steam navigation came to be monopolized by the English and it worked as main instrument for controlling Indian economy. It was not till 1906 that the Muslim Merchants of Bombay, headed by Adamji Peerbhoy, formed shipping company which acquired nine steamships. But after a number of accidents, the enterprise failed.[27] Thereafter, the creation of a modern mercantile marine was again postponed for several decades.

The inland trade, which the Gujaratis carried on, was mainly concentrated in Gujarat and Maharashtra. However, in the 19th century, their trading activities spread also to the other parts of India, particularly the south. The Parsis, for example, controlled the major part of the maritime trade of Karnataka and Kerala already in the early years of the last century and began to settle there in increasing number after the British occupied these regions. Besides Parsis, Banias from Gujarat and Marwaris also emigrated to the Karnataka and Kerala during the period.[28]

The activity of sub-contractors engaged in ship building was also of considerable importance. In the thirties of the 18th century, the East India Company set up a shipyard in Bombay. The first shipbuilding establishment of the East India Company on the West Coast was, in Surat where from 1673 onwards, the Parsis built vessel for the Company. In 1735, an officer taking over a ship constructed in the shipyard of Surat was struck by the skill and knowledge of the shipwright Lowji Nushirvanji and suggested to him that he should take charge of the work at the docks which were at that time, under construction in Bombay.[29] According to Maria Graham, who visited Jamshed Bakhman, the great grandson of Lowji in 1839, Lawji Nashirvanji came to Gujarat to work in the dock-yard as a day labourer and it was due to his great ability that he became a shipwright.[30] In 1742, Lowji applied for a loan of Rs. 1,000 to Council of Bombay for merit and loyalty. When he died in 1774, he left a house and £ 3,000 to his heirs. [31] He was ancestor of the Wadia's family from which came many leading shipbuilders of Bombay and later on, at the close of the 19th century a number of big industrialists.

Lowji's grandsons, Manekji and Bakhmanji, who died in 1790 and 1792 respectively, did not manage to leave large fortune to their sons, Framji Maneckji and Jamshedji Bakhmanji, who succeeded them.[32] C. R. Low referred to the great services of J. Bakhmanji who began to build ships of the line in the shipyards of Bombay.[33]

In 1802, he launched the frigate 'Cornwallis' which was the signal for East India Company to embark on a feverish building programme of big men-of-war, that were launched in the dockyards of Bombay. The information as to the conditions in which the Indian capitalists participated in the work of the shipyard is rather incomplete. It seems that the docks were, either entirely or to a considerable extent, the property of East India Company. In any case, there is no indication of any Indian dock-owners. However, it can be said with certainty that Indians who played a part in the shipbuilding industry were not merely workers and foremen. Even the size of the inheritance left by Lowji Nushirvanji Wadia indicates that he was probably a contractor. Lowji's great grandsons owned a large tract of land in Bombay. Maria Graham wrote in 1809, "Pestongee (a brother of J. Bakhmanji) told me that he received not less than of £ 15,000 a year in rents, and that his brother received nearly as much.:[34] Postans, an English woman, who visited the Wadia family thirty years after Maria Graham, relates that the splendor of Lowji's castle astonished her. In the course of his conversation with her the master of the house mentioned his extensive trade with China and referred to the cost of the valuable cargo which had just been brought to Bombay in one of his own ships. He then observed that the Parsis were greatly indebted to the Europeans for the help they received from them at the start of their commercial activities.[35]

The Asiatic Journal of 1838 reported that many Parsi craftsmen who began work in shipyard of Bombay as ordinary workers had become rich shipbuilders through their own skill and enterprise.[36] This undoubtedly also refers to the numerous members of the Wadia family. A question worth examining in this connection is that if the dockyards belonged entirely to the East India Company what role did the Indian capitalists play in that? It should be kept in mind that a considerable field remained open to private native initiative. According to W. Hamilton, the shipyards were full of Parsis who had gained monopoly in all departments. The supplier of timber was a Parsi, as was the man who inspected the finished ships.[37] The supply of timber for the shipyards was indeed in the hands of Parsi merchants. A copy of an agreement for the supply of timber signed as early as 1741 by the representative of the Company and the Parsi Bhikha Ratan and Runju Dhanji is still in existence.[38]

The shipyards of Bombay were a capitalist enterprise, the fixed capital of which belonged to the East India Company and the circulating capital to native capitalist contractors.[39] An official document regarding the shipbuilding activities in Bombay states that the number of ship built during 1805-14 was 38 while during 1855 and 1856 the number of ships built in Bombay was just 1 and 2 respectively.[40] The vessels built in Bombay were notable for their great sea worthiness and strength. C. R, Low quotes a letter written by the chief officer of a frigate hailing from Bombay to his builder Jamshedjee Bomanjee. The letter relates that a fleet of seventeen British ships spent the winter of 1808-09, in extremely difficult ice conditions, in the Baltic Sea and that only the frigate which was built in Bombay escaped serious damage.[41]

The battleship Asia carrying 84 guns and having displacement of 2883 tons was launched in the shipyard of Bombay in 1824. It was the biggest men-of-war ever to have been built there. After the ship had taken part in the battle of Navarino, Admiral P. Malcolm sent a message to her builder Nowroji Jamshedji informing him that the battleship Asia had played a major role in the naval engagement and that the admiral was proud of the success of her builder.[42] The high quality of the ships launched in Bombay was not only due to the skill of the Parsi shipwrights but to a considerable extent also to the excellent timber used in their construction.

In 1838, the first steamship 'Snake' was built in the docks of Bombay followed by 'Victoria' and a river boat with a displacement of 204 tons. Between 1838 and 1857, a total of 21 steamships were built in Bombay. The biggest of these were the steam frigates, 'Assaye' and 'Punjab' with a displacement of 1800 tons each, built in 1854.[43]

From the above account, it becomes clear that Bombay had the potential for becoming an important shipbuilding centre of sea-going vessels but the shipyards of Bombay remained subordinated to the interest of the English from the very beginning. So for as the East India Company was concerned, it could take its advantage by building for its own requirements goods and cheap vessels in India, especially as they brought in big profits. After the abolition of the East India Company, the British capitalists took up direct control over India and they found a dangerous competitor to their interest in the form of Bombay shipyards. Hence they discontinued the shipbuilding activities in Bombay after 1857. The steam vessels were no longer built at all in Bombay while only a few small coasting vessels were launched.[44] The closer of Bombay shipbuilding was not just because of economic considerations, as the Bombay built ships were much cheaper. In fact, the British Government wanted to deprive India of her shipbuilding facilities, and to establish a British monopoly of maritime transport. The British capitalist succeeded very much in their this attempt. Had India been free at the time, the Bombay shipbuilding activity would have developed into a fully fledged industry.

The merchants of Bombay also largely profited from the real estate they owned in the town. According to Maria Graham, "The Parsis are the chief landholders in Bombay. Almost all the houses and gardens inhabited by the European are their property."[45]

During the first half of the 19th century, extremely favorable conditions existed for the collaboration of big Guajarati merchants with British industrial capital. The field in which this collaboration existed included broking in commercial transaction, export of opium, credit operations, shipbuilding and other industries in Bombay. Perhaps, no other group of Indian merchants established such a firm and cordial relations with the colonists as the group of Bombay merchant did. It was because of this only that the merchants of Bombay were able to build industrial enterprises earlier than those in other parts of the country and this led subsequently to an intensification of contradictions between them and the British.

Now let us examine the role played by Marwari traders and money lenders in the first half of the 19th century Bombay. The accomplishment of industrial revolution in England enabled the British industrial capital to turn the whole of India into a market for its industrial product. Moreover, under the British the taxation became heavier and the export of agricultural commodities *i.e.* cotton, jute an indigo began on massive scale. The transformation of Indian peasants into a small commodity producer created additional opportunity for peasant's slavery by the money lenders. The occurrence of natural calamity and extraordinary expenses of the peasent household also led to the money lending class to their exploitation either during commercial transaction or by lending him money. The former system of feudal tax farming came to be replaced by a new system of exploiting the peasents by means of commerce and money lending. The primary unit of this new form of exploitation was the village trader and money lender. The very fact that this local network of trading and money lending capital was so widespread that it created favorable conditions for a new mass emigration of member of the Marwari caste from Rajputana. During the first half of the 19th century Rajputana was by no means an ideal place for large scale trading and money lending operations. No provisions for the safety of life and property existed there. The activities of big trading and money lending firms at the beginning of the 19th century continued to include the carrying of goods and money from one place to another place protected by armed detachments which they hired by granting of loans to Princes at high interest rates, and active participation in the commerce with neighboring regions.

Although local trade was relatively brisk, its volume remained fairly constant and thus afforded only limited scope for merchant capital. The trading and money lending capital of Rajputana went therefore beyond its borders in search of new opportunities provided by the English capitalists. The mass emigration of traders and money lenders from Rajputana was connected with their attempt to make use of the new conditions created by the English colonialists.

T. R. Sharma, an economist, wrote that the Marwaris originally inhabited a small district in the neighborhood of the town of Nawalgarh and Pilani on the river Shekhavati, in Rajputana, north of Jaipur. After the establishment of British rule, their desire for profit took them to almost all parts of India, especially to the industrial and trading centers such as Calcutta.

Maharashtra, where the cultivation of cotton led during this period to a considerable development of commodity-money relations in the countryside, became the object of special attention of Marwari traders and moneylenders. The advance of the Marwari's in Maharashtra can be traced especially on the basis of the data on the immigration into the Western part of the region, where almost no petty Marwari money lenders lived before the 19th century. For example, in the Nasik District, the Marwari's made their appearance in the first quarter of the 19th century.[46] As regards Poona, the Bombay Gazetteer informs us that the Marwar Vanis came later than the Gujaratis, but were settled in the district in large numbers before the beginning of British rule.[47] The majority of Marwaris who lives in Ahmednagar District arrived there after the establishment of British power. The Gazetteer of Sholapur District mentioned in 1844 that the Marwari's immigrated there about fifty years earlier.

One question that arises in this context is that how did members of the Marwari community of traders and money lenders migrate to all parts of India as a result of the establishment of colonial rule? The reason behind this was that the British industrial capital required the co-operation of the indigenous trading and money lending capital in order to exploit the conquered country. For this purpose the trading and money lending capital had to have an organization that was sufficiently widespread, so that every peasent household could be caught in its network. At the same time, it was to be sufficiently centralized to enable British capital, which had attained a high degree of concentration by means of commerce and money lending to exploit the working people of India. The peasents both as producers and sellers of raw materials and as consumers of British commodities. In the rural economy of colonial India, such a system was based on the trading and financial and commercial organization of the trading and money lending caste, whose members formed a complicated hierarchy starting from the petty village traders and money lender upto the big city merchant and banker. The castes were firmly held together by credit arrangements and financial relations that had developed between caste members. The trading and money lending groups constituting the Marwari community were best suited to meet the needs of British capital not only because they formed the largest organization of Indian traders and money lenders, apart from the Gujarati Banias, but also because Marwari bankers were already established in almost every towns of north India at the time the country was conquered.

The nature of business transaction of the Marwaris was broking or to act as middlemen, which played proportionally smaller part in the business activities of Marwari trading and money lending capital than in those of the merchant of Bombay or the Gujarati merchants in general. The reason was that the Marwaris carried on their business chiefly in remote parts of the country where the volume of the home trade was far greater than amounts involved in the commercial deals in which they collaborated with the British. In addition, they continued to engage, although to a diminishing extent, in the monetary, commercial and financial operations which were customary in feudal India.

Jenkins, an Englishman, who visited Nagpur in 1823, writes to the Council of East India Company, "Most of the

Sawkars in this part of the country are Marwaris. There are only two banking houses in the city conducted by Brahmins (Maratha Brahmins). It is difficult to enumerate and describe their various speculations."[48] Jenkin also lays stress on such operations as money changing, remittance of money, commerce in gold, silver and precious stones. However, activities of Marwaris were not confined to monetary and commercial transactions only. Jenkins writes: "Their country business is, besides the common affairs of money exchanging, to advance cash on grains to Patels and ryots. For the later purpose, some have large stores of grains, for the loan of which they take 25 per cent for eight month, the time of repayment being usually at the harvest. They may also lend money to artisans and merchants."[49]

The Gazetteer of Bombay City and Island informs us about two classes of money lenders operating in Bombay one professional money lender and other casual money lender.[50] The casual money lenders used to lend money to their friends at the rate of 6 per cent to 9 per cents and frequently failed to obtain a receipt from the borrower and had to prove their case, if it came out in court, almost wholly by oral evidence. The professional money lender may be either one who wholly subsists on money lending or combines with some other profession or trade. "At the head of the first class stands the Marwari, at the head of the second Danavala or grain seller who, in addition to selling different grains at a very heavy price, lends money to his customers at a high rate of interest. There are also a certain number of Parsis and Deccan Hindus, who, having themselves been at one time victims of the Marwari, have now adopted his line of business on their own account."[51] Regarding the modus operandi of the Marwari moneylenders Gazetteer states that "The Marwari's chief weapon is the blank penalty note. In addition to the regular promissory note promising to repay about three or four or sometimes even five times the amount advanced with interest at 75 per cent per annum on inflated loan, the borrower is induced to put his signature, with a statement that a certain sum has been borrowed, across a receipt stamped at the foot of a paper the upper part of which is blank, on the understanding that it will be returned when the amount of the original note is paid off. Sometimes, it is so returned but at other time if the debtor goes to the insolvency court or otherwise defrauds the Marwadi the later fills in the blank note if necessary with a date subsequent to the insolvency and files a suit on it. This is called a penalty note."[52] The Marwaris generally maintain three sets of account books. His genuine book of accounts never comes in court, and his customers are drawn from all classes and range from the expectant heir down to the mill hands.

The Danawalas or grain merchant's opportunity lies in the fact that in a crowded city like Bombay people do not have the space to stock grain in large quantities. Therefore, they have an account with Danawala, who also lends them money. His accounts are never balanced, so that he can insert or temper with entries in any way he likes. His chief customers are mill hands and as this dealing with them are on credit and the risk great; he considers himself entitled to charge to the account of one customer the payment of another. To him all mill hands are alike; Khatrawalas or cart-drivers are also good customers of his and their belongings are mostly mortgaged with him or with the Marwari.

The overthrow of the Peshwa's rule in Maharashtra by the British and the creation of new condition for exploitation led the big bankers and merchants to suffer heavy losses because their best customers the Peshwa state and the great feudal lords were crushed. But when the British Government imposed the excessive land tax to be paid in cash, and destroyed the village community it made the Maratha peasents to be dependent upon the money lenders. Since the tax was collected either before the harvest began or directly after its completion, the peasents had not enough time to sell their products. If they did manage to sell them they could only get the low prices prevailing at the time of the year. To pay the land tax in time, the ryot was, therefore, inevitably forced to borrow from the money lender.[53] The ryotwari land tax system which the British introduced in Maharashtra accelerated the enslavement of the peasents by the money lenders. To be able to pay their taxes the peasents had to sell their cotton and wheat, the principal marketable products of the rural economy to the money-lender.[54] Thus, the peasent's dependence on trading and money lending capital increased further. But in the twenties and also partly in the thirties of the 19th century, the British rule obstructed the activities of the money lending capital as it appropriated not only the surplus product but also part of the necessary product. It is significant that the first big influx of Marwaris into Thana District on the sea-coast opposite Bombay, occurred in connection with the sharp decrease of tax in 1835-37, which made land valuable.[55]

No documentary evidence exists showing that Marwari money lenders were ruined. It seems that the Marwari's were able to adjust themselves to the conditions existing in Maharashtra during the period of transition, when the old system of feudal exploitation was already wrecked and the system of colonial oppression, which made use of commercial and money capital and of the ramnants of feudalism surviving in the countryside began to take shape. Over "the increasing penetration of small traders and money lenders into the villages during the first half of the 19th century prepared Marwari capital for the role it was to play as agents of British capital when India was exploited by Imperialist methods."[56]

During the first half of 19th century, the big Indian merchants and money lenders continued to act as reliable political supporters of the British, Lt. Col. W. H. Sleeman, who served in India for many years remarked: "There is no class of men more interested in the stability of our rule in India than that of the respectable merchants, nor is there any upon whom the welfare of our government, and of the people, more depends."[57]

Many big Indian traders independent of their nationality and caste continued to serve the British during the national uprising. The Gazetteers of those districts of the United Provinces that were affected by the revolt were full of reports about loyalty of the top strata of the native merchants and moneylenders. For their services during the national uprising like making available money and provision to the British, for which, many traders and money lenders were rewarded with estates and titles.[58] Among the recipients of this reward was Abhirchand Daga. However, it should not be taken for granted that all Indian merchants sided with the British.

Indrabhan, the founder of the firm of Bansilal Abhirchand, came to Western Maharashtra about 1820, *i.e.* soon after it was conquered by the British. Together with his brother Bansilal he opened a shop in Amravati where he traded in grain and later on began to lend money as well. Their money lending operations enabled the brothers to build up a stock of grain and Bansilal was selling grain to the British army before the Indian national uprising of 1857-59. Bansilal's son was granted the title Raibahadur for the assistance he rendered to British punitive detachments during the uprising. The same title was conferred on the younger son of Bansilal, who supplied the British army with provisions during the second Anglo-Afgan war of 1878-80. The members of Bansilal Abirchand's family grew rich as a result of making deliveries to the British army and subsequently became the great bankers in Maharashtra.[59]

The founder of the firm of Mohta began his business activity in the cotton growing region of the Central Provinces in the thirties of the 19th century. His son Raikchand expanded the cotton and grain business and seized the lands or many villages. He was the first Marwari to build a cotton mill, and later on second. In addition Mohta owned ten cotton processing enterprises.[60]

Thus, the exploitation of India by imperialist methods led to substantial changes in the business activities of the Marwaris. The Marwaris began to participate in the export of cotton and other raw materials to England, and in the sale of British cloth and other industrial commodities. This type of trade did not form a sufficiently large proportion of the total trade turnover in the interior regions to allow us to assume that the majority of local Marwari dealers acted chiefly as intermediaries of the British. Apart from the colonial centers, the commerce of the Marwaris catered mainly to the internal commodity exchange. But the role played by Marwari capital within the system of colonial exploitation should not be underestimated. The more so in a number of cases the internal commodity exchange served the requirements of foreign capital, for instance, the supply of foodstuffs to the cotton and jute growing areas and to the tea plantations.

Because the Marwari merchant, especially those in the colonial centers, were involved in the commercial transactions that served the British and since their investments in the national industry were quite insignificant, separate groups of Marwari capitalists projected their own narrow interest against the test of the Indian capitalists.

The colonial conditions in Maharashtra as well as in Bombay, thus, provided only very limited opportunities for the creation of large scale capitalist industry. However, the Marwari trading and money lending capital did not make use of the limited opportunities, since collaboration with the colonialists provided it with a sufficiently high rate of profit. The cotton mills existing in Maharashtra therefore belonged either to Gujarati Parsis or British capitalists.

An episode of J. N. Tata is significant in this connection In 1876, when he was building cotton mill in Nagpur he required money for the construction of a dam. He turned to a local Marwari moneylender and suggested that the later should become the shareholder of the company but the Marwari refused saying that it did not benefit him. The investment of Marwari capital in Industrial enterprises for the initial processing of agricultural raw materials was in fact a supplement or continuation of their commercial and money lending activities and did not involve considerable expenditure, since these enterprises required little fixed capital.

During the latter half of the 19th century, the Marwari merchants took advantage of the growing dependence of the producer on loans and the supply of machine made semi-finished products which were mostly imported, such as yarn, metals and dyes to strengthen their control over the principal branches of manufacture. In this respect, the Marathas and Gujarati merchants and money lenders did not lag behind Marwaris. At the close of the 19th century, the Marwaris who had wide opportunities to obtain loans gained a firm hold on the handicrafts in Maharashtra. The domination of the money-lenders over the handicraft industries retarded the development of the higher forms of capitalist enterprise and condemned the small produces to an exceedingly painful expropriation.

The Marwaris were engaged in widespread financial and money lending transactions and occupied prominent positions as brokers in the wholesale trade of the towns. Among indigenous bankers in Bombay were no doubt Marwari bankers too. This is confirmed by the fact that their commercial operations were directed towards Rajputana and Central India. In fact, very little is known about the scale and nature of the business activities of the Marwari capitalists in Bombay even at the close of the 19th and the early 20th century.

From the above account it follows that the big Gujarati merchants collaborated and highly co-operated with the British capitalists in order to gain accumulation of their capital. They were very successful also in their venture and through their mercantile activities in cotton and opium as well as shipbuilding industry they amassed a good deal of wealth. But in the first half of the 19th century they could not play any leading role in the capitalistic enterprises because, although they were numerically stronger in number to the Europeans, the native merchant capital always remained subordinated to the British industrial capital. It was true that some of the Parsis did invest in shipbuilding activity where they had the potential to grow but the Europeans closed down the industry by 1857 as they found a great rival to them in the form of native merchants.

So far as the role of money lending capital was concerned it has become very clear from the above account that unlike the other merchants the Marwaris were not at all interested in investing into the capitalistic enterprises for they remained confined to their usarious business only. Although they made full use of the colonial conditions created by the British for amassing wealth, they showed reluctance in capitalistic investment. Consequently, their capital too could not play any major role even by the end of the 19th century.

REFERENCES

1. The value of Bombay's export and import (in million rupees) 1800-1809, 1810-1819, 1820-1829, 1830-1839, 1840-1849, 1850-1859, 56.0 46.7 56.6 82.2 192.4 262.0 *G.B.C.I. (Bombay, 1909)*, Vol. I, p. 416.
2. J. Malcom: *Memoir of Central India including Malwa and adjoining provinces (London, 1832)* II, III. 2.
3. Maria Graham: *Journal of the Residence in India (Edinburg, 1813)*, pp. 32-33.
4. The Present Commerce in cotton between Berar and Bombay was originated, and is chiefly carried on, by native merchants (J. Chapman: *The Cotton and Commerce of India (London, 1860)*, p.15.
5. *Ibid.*
6. *Ibid.*, p. 90.
7. A. K. Forbes: *Rasmala*, II, p. 248.
8. *Ibid.*
9. Postans: *Western India in 1838 (London, 1838)*, II, pp. 222, 223.
10. The East India Company received seven shillings, six pence from each pound of opium sold in Calcutta in the middle of the nineteenth century and transit duties levied on opium from Malwa brought the company five shillings eight pence per pound.

    (I. W. Kaye: *The Administration of the East India Company: A History of India's Progress (London, 1853)*, p. 683.

    Duties imposed on opium rose from 125 Rs. Per chest in 1835, 42 to Rs. 700/- in 1862. *Quoted by* V. I. Pavlov *in The Indian Capitalist Class (New Delhi, 1999)*, p. 144.
11. Turner: *The Indian Textile Journal (February, 1931)*, pp. 55, 56.
12. *Proceedings of Indian History Congress, (Kurukshetra, 1983)*, Vol. 43, p. 512 (Hereafter to be referred as PHIC.).

13. *Ibid.*
14. William Milburn: *Oriental Commerce (1813)*, Vol. I, p. 234.
15. S. M. Edwardes: *Rise of Bombay*, p. 163.
16. Milburn: *Op.cit.*, Vol. I, p. 234.
17. D. E. Wacha: *Shells from the Sands of ...*, p. 416.
18. *Ibid.*, p. 427.
19. S. H. Jhabvala: *Sir Jamshedji Jeejeebhoy, Baronet (Bombay)*, p. 20.
20. Postans: *Op. cit.*, Vol. I, p. 122.
21. J. Chapman: *Op.cit.*, p. 75.
22. Postans: *Op.cit.*, Vol. I, p. 122.
23. W. H. Coates: *The Old Country Trade*, p. 52.
24. *Ibid.*, p. 59.
25. Dr. R. R. Singh: *'Opium Trade of Bombay in the 19th Century' in P.I.H.C. (Kurukshetra, 1983)*, Vol. 43, p. 512.
26. *Ibid.*, p. 150-160.
27. *Ibid.*
28. A. Sarda Raju: *Economic Conditions in the Madras Presidency: 1800-1815 (Madras, 1941)*, p. 188.
29. *Handbook for India (Bombay-1859), Part-II*, p. 279.
30. Maria Graham: *Journal of the Residence in India (1813)*, pp. 32, 33.
31. *Material towards the Statistical Account of the Town and Island of Bombay-I (History), (G.B.C.I., XXVI), Bombay 1893*, p. 191.
32. G. B.C.I., Vol. I, P-391.
33. C. R. Low: *History of the Indian Navy (London-1877) –II*, p. 17.
34. Graham: *Op.cit.*, p. 45.
35. Postans: *Op.cit., I*, p. 106.
36. G. B. C. I. *(Bombay, 1909)*, Vol. II, p. 149.
37. W. Hamilton: *East India Gazetteer (London, 1828)*, I, p. 261.
38. *Ibid.*, p. 190.
39. V. I. Pavlov: *The Indian Capitalist Class (New Delhi, 1999)*, p. 124.
40. *Ibid.*
41. C. R. Low: *History of the Indian Navy, (London-1877)* Vol. I, p. 279-298.

42. *Ibid.*, Vol. II, p. 4.

43. *Ibid.*

44. *Ibid.* I, pp. 540-541.

45. Maria Graham: *Op.cit.*, p. 45.

46. *Nasik (G.B.C.I., XVI)*, p. 44.

47. *Poona (G.B.C.I., XVII, Pt.2; Bombay 1885)*, p. 99.

48. *Central Provinces Provincial Banking Inquiry Committee (Nagpur, 1930)*, Vol. I, p. 333.

49. *Ibid.*, p. 334.

50. *G.B.C.I. (1909)*, p. 303.

51. *Ibid.*

52. *Ibid.* p. 304.

53. R.D. Choksey: *Economic History of the Bombay Decean*, p. 107.

54. *Ibid.*, p. 309.

55. *Thana (G.B.C.I., VIII, Pt. I; Bombay, 1882)*, p. 308.

56. V.I. Pavlov: *Op.cit., (New Delhi, 1999)*, p. 134.

57. *Ibid.*, p. 135.

58. *District Gazetteers of the United Provinces, (Allahabad, 1909 1911).*

59. *Central Provinces Provincial Banking Enquiry Committee-II.* p. 497.

60. *Ibid.*

5

Comprador Nature of Indian Industrial Capitalists

(1851 – 1900 A.D.)

In modern time, there have been vigorous studies in the origin and growth of early entrepreneurship in India, particularly in the port cities like Bombay, Calcutta and Madras. During 1910-1915, Max Weber studied entrepreneurship and put forth theories regarding the development of entrepreneurship among some communities of India. In the *first* theory, he emphasized entrepreneur's pariah aspect, which implied the political and social dispriviledge's of entrepreneur groups such as Parsis, Jews, and some of the great Hindu merchant castes like the Banias who have been called the 'Jews of India.'[1] In *second* theory, he established an analogy between the theory of the Protestant ethic and Jainism and Vallabhacharya sect of Vaishnavism. About the Jains, he says: "The compulsory saving of asceticism familiar from the economic history of Puritanism worked also among them, the Jains, towards the use of accumulated possessions, as investment capital rather than as a fund for consumption or rent." About Vallabhacharya sect of Vaishnavism, he says that Banias of this sect found the mildly hedonistic sect to their liking as they were alive to find a taste for the service of God. "An extraordinary large member of them belonged to this somewhat socially exclusive sect."[2]

Bombay's early entrepreneurs were Parsis, Jews, Jains, Kapol and Bhatia Banias hence Max Weber's both theories can be applied for the explanation of early entrepreneurship in Bombay city. Even the emergence of entrepreneurs among Bombay's Gujarati, Muslim communities like the Khojas, the Memons and the Bohras can also be explained in terms of Max Weber's above mentioned theories.

Max Weber's theories, however, cannot be spared from exceptions. As a citation of few exceptions, it can be pointed out that whereas the Bagdadi Jews, the Sassoons in Bombay emerged as entrepreneurs the Bene-Israil Jews in Bombay, migrated from the Colaba district, remained mariners, carpenters, mechanics, draftsmen, surveyors and clerks.[3] The Konkani Muslims, who were originally Arabs, played very important role in Bombay's coastal and foreign trade but not in industrial ventures. Moreover, within Bombay Presidency, at Ahmadabad Ranchodlal a Brahmin, floated a cotton mill as early as 1848.[4] Above all the idea of cotton mill in Bombay was mooted by Dr. Bhau Daji, a Saraswat Brahmin in 1840s.[5]

Of late the economic historians have carried on further researches on this subject in general as well as case study related to some entrepreneurial communities in India. D. R. Gadgil[6], Ashok V. Desai[7], Amiya Kumar Bagchi[8], Russian' scholars V.I. Pavlov, I.L. Reuinser and G.K. Shirkov[9] and others have carried on general studies. The scholars like Bekehard Kuleke[10], Thomas Timberg[11]. Amlendu Guha[12] and others have carried on case study of different business communities in India.

In all above mentioned studies, the general tendency has been to attribute entrepreneurship to traditional Hindu trading castes like Banias and trading communities like Jain, Parsi, Jew, Khoja, Memon, Bohra and the like. But the facts indicate that the majority of the people of these castes and communities remained petty shopkeepers and traders. Hence it is more appropriate to study the emergence of entrepreneurship in some family of different communities rather than to attribute it to the whole community. This is the conclusion Milton Singer has reached from his study of Chettiar money lender and business community of Tamilnadu.[13] Thomas Timberg also emphasizes: "Even within a commercial community, it was only some businessmen who involved themselves in industrial entrepreneurship."[14] Discounting even joint family as the basis for entrepreneurship R.S. Rungta asserts" "Though there was nothing to stop a joint family from promoting corporate enterprise it offered a large enough scope to satisfy the ambition of most ordinary individuals, particularly those with the limited vision of life."[15]

Mrs. D.P. Pandit, in her study of the rise of entrepreneurship in the Western India, stresses the primary region and new influences, which made merchants of the port city of Bombay the innovator.[16] K.I. Gillion supports this point of view in his study of Ahmadabad city.[17] Mrs. Hemlata Acharya.[18] and R.S. Rungta[19] rejects Mrs. Pandit's assertion and emphasize the availability of economic opportunities in the region as the basis of this development. R.S. Rungta asserts: "Banias were the trading community among the Hindus all over India. Nobody in Rajasthan calls a person known in Calcutta as Marwari. In Rajasthan a Marwari is called a Bania. The term Marwari, Sindhi, Gujarati, as business class, were attached to the Banias in other part. Why some of the Banias from certain parts became well known should be sought more in the type of economic opportunities available in the region of their settlement rather than any other factor."[20]

The Soviet Scholar, V.I. Pavlov, L.I. Ruinser and G.K. Shirkov[21] and Indian scholar, Amlendu Guha[22] have recently put forth the theory of *comprador capitalist* who collaborated with the British and gained concessions of trade and consequently amassed vast wealth which they transferred to the new lines of endeavor, *viz.*, industrial enterprises. These scholars thus emphasize economic basis for the rise of entrepreneurship, which, however, does not reject other factors such as Pariah, and puritan ethnic basis, trading community-basis, economic opportunities basis, and even region basis.

The comprador theory can be applied for the analysis of

the emergence of Parsi entrepreneurship in Bombay city in the middle of the 19th century. Most of the early entrepreneurs in Bombay city were connected with the East India Company and European business houses as contractors, brokers and Dubhas (interpreters). For instance, the first entrepreneur of textile industry in Bombay city was Cawasji Nanabhai Davar (1818-73), who set up first successful cotton mill in the city of Bombay. He belonged to the family of brokers to the British firms and has himself worked as broker to some of the British firms.[23]

Maneckji Nasservanji Petit, who floated the second cotton mill, also belonged to the family of Dubhas (interpreter) and commission agent to the French and Dutch ships and he himself was broker to a number of European firms in 1840s and early 1850.[24]

The leading Jain mill owner of 1870, Nursey Keshowji, also belonged to family of brokers.[25] Kapol Bania mill-owner, Varjivan Das Madhav Das belonged to a family of contractor and supplier of corn to the East India Company.[26] He also acted as a guarantee broker to a European firm.[27]

The exceptions can be cited to this theory also as many entrepreneurs in the second half of the nineteenth century were independent businessmen. Gokluldas Tejpal, Luxmidas Khimji and others were independent businessmen. Thackersey Moolji, who emerged as biggest mill-owner in Hindu community, was also an independent businessman. It, however, cannot be denied that all these independent businessman were well designed to the British rulers and had close connection with British business houses. It was this relationship which made Lieutenant Colonel W.H. Sleeman to remark "There is no class of men more interested in the stability of our rule in India than that of the respectable merchants, nor is there any upon whom the welfare of our government and of the people more depends."[28]

As has already been stated earlier that during the first half of the 19th century a very favourable condition existed for the collaboration of the big Gujarati merchant capital with British

Industrial capital. The fields in which these collaborative activities took place were the broking in commercial transactions, export of opium, credit operations, shipbuilding and other industries in Bombay. In no other parts of India, the native merchants established such a good and cordial relationship with the British capitalists and this was most probably the reason why the merchants of Bombay were successful in building industrial enterprises in Bombay much earlier than even at Calcutta or any other city under the colonial rule. The Khatris of Chaul who had migrated to Bombay in 1600 A. D. due to the outbreak of plague at Chaul, started in Bombay some sort of hand industry of silk cloth making and Chapa and Chanderi work. They continued with their traditional profession under the Portuguese rule and then under the East India Company and their profession flourished due to the increasing economic activities and developing trade which made some of them very rich.[29]

As early as 1676, a regular cotton industry (hand industry) was established in Bombay. A letter from Surat factory to Bombay, dated 4th November 1676 States: "We are assured if you and your brokers there would be as industrious as you ought in inviting and encouraging weavers to settle with you, that manufacture of calicoes would be increased much more than it is. We desire therefore seriously and earnestly to take this affair into your consideration and to use all just means possible to invite and encourage weavers of all sorts to inhabit on the Island. It is our opinion that seeing the country of Shivaji and Deccan as harassed and much ruined by the wars, if you did employ some persons to invite the weavers of these parts to come over to you, they would gladly accept it only for a secure livelihood sake. Wherefore use your endeavors herein, we give you notice that it is the Company's particular direction to us to procure as many as Dangri weavers to settle on the Island as we can in regard that commodity is in request to whom and also we would have you procured as many Pautka weavers as you can, for they will also be necessary and assure yourselves what industry and ingenuity you employ in this affair will be well esteemed by your Hon'ble Masters and ourselves. For your better supply of cotton yarn for keeping said weavers at work, we shall send you down a considerable parcel of Rajapur yarn, which will be with you in a few days after receipt of this letter, where of what is proper to be delivered out to the weavers for the making of any sort of calicoes fit for Europe above mentioned we would have you so disposed of and the remainder be sold to the Company's best advantages."[30] By the close of the seventeenth century, Bombay Island witnessed some more entrepreneurial activities. In 1683, it was decided to establish a manufacture of knitted stockings in Bombay.[31] Around the same time, Cawasji Cama, an ancestor of the illustrious family of Lawji Narsurwanji Wadia moved to Bombay from Surat at the instance of the Bombay Factors and established the shipbuilding industry. After some time, Rustomji Dorabji also established shipbuilding industry in the island as a result of which, he was appointed the Patel of Bombay Government.[32]

During 1724-25, Cawasji Rustomji visited England and brought back 12 pin coils and 3 stills and started making alcoholic drinks in 1780s.[33] Further R.V. Wadia and D. Dadiseth started wine making and distinguished themselves as master shipbuilders in Bombay. S. M. Edwardes opines that early references of shipping at Bombay are few.[34] The shipbuilding in Bombay developed into a fine art not until 1735 when Lawji Nasurwanji Wadia was brought down from Surat and bidden to open trade in teak with Bhils and wild tribes on the Island forest.[35] Then he declares that "The ships at Bombay comprised beautiful modeled English build galleys.:[36] Naturally enough Bombay shipbuilding followed the line of Surat shipbuilding.[37] This indicates that it ows little or nothing to England.

The family of Lawji Nasurwanji Wadia dominated the shipbuilding activities at the Bombay Dockyard for a century and half (1736 to 1884) and built over 350 vessels grab sloops, pilot vessels, frigates, gunboats and steamers for the navy as well as for private owners.[38] Among these were some of the finest sailing ships that ever rode the seas. The battleship Asia built in 1824 by Nawrojee Jamsetji, the Fourth Master Builder of the Bombay Dockyard, distinguished itself as the flagship of Admiral Cordington in battle of Navarino (1827) in which the Anglo-Greek alliance destroyed the Turkish and Egyptian fleets.

In 1829, the yard built its first steamship, 'Hugh Lindsay' which helped to establish the practicability of running steamer service between India and Suez. With closing of the Bombay Marine, the Dockyard lost its importance; ending with it the career of some of the finest craftsmen in shipbuilding in India.[39] Yet in its heyday the Bombay built ships were superior to European built ships in many ways. They were so strong that they were successfully used by the Royal Navy and earned in 1811 the following appreciation from Col. Walker: "Many ships Bombay built after running 14 to 15 years have been brought into navy and were considered as strong as ever. Sir Edmond Huges performed, I believe eight voyages as an India man before she was purchased by the navy. No European built India man is capable of going more than six voyages with safety."[40]

From 1735 to 1835, the Bombay shipyard built 267 ships with a displacement of 23 to 2298 tons, of these 30 ships had displacement of over 1,000 tons and four 2,000 tons. The first steamer as stated above was built in Bombay in 1829 (displacement 411 tons). In 1838, a river steamboat with an iron bull, the 'Snake' with displacement of 40 tons, was built in Bombay. It was followed in 1839 by the first sloop, the Victoria (705 tons) and a 204 ton river steamboat. Altogether from 1833 to 1857, 21 steamships were built in Bombay, the biggest of these being two steam frigates, the Assaye and the Punjab with a displacement of 1800 tons each.[41] it is however difficult to explain why the British government later on closed down the Bombay shipyard. "The East India Company found profitable to build good and cheap ships in India, especially since this yielded a large income. When the Company began to wind up, British industrial bourgeoisie having obtained direct control over India, hastened to put an end to the Bombay shipyard which it regarded only as a rival to it."[42]

Apart from the shipbuilding industry the Parsis manufactured gunpowder for East India Company. In 1677,

Munjee Dhunji of Surat received Company's contract to construct in Bombay the first large gunpowder works. From 1740s to 1780s, the famous gun-powder maker was Manakjee Manuwah. After him, his sons were the gun-powder makers in the eightees of the eighteenth century. In 1797, Bomanji Hirji was the supplier of gunpowder and in 1840; Merwanji Rustomji enjoyed the same position.[43]

In 1808, a Parsi Pallonjee Bomanjee set up a carriage making works in Bombay with an initial capital of Rs. 5000/- and assumed the name of P.B. Pankhiwala. Very soon, he grew rich and his workshop became a large establishment run on capitalist lines. He paid his workers Rs. 15 to 20 per month and manufactured European type of carriages for export to Europe, Singapore and Afghanistan.[44]

There were sweetmeat manufacturing shops in Bombay at very early times and the oldest sweetmeat manufacturer was Amichand Govindji who established his business about the year 1779 at Boribunder at a spot then known as the Three Gates.[45] One of the best known bakeries of old time was established in about 1809 by a Goanes in old Hanuman Cross Lane[46] and one of the first Bidi making and selling shop was opened by a Brahmin on Erskine road in 1836.[47] There is another account that a Khoja started Bidi making and selling shop at Worli as early as 1784.[48] Then there were many other hand industry like basket making. Hooka making, leaf-fan making etc., at early times in the city.

The first attempt to set up a textile mill was made by Cawasji Nanabhai Davar in 1854. Sorabji Shappurji a former forman in the East India Company's cannon works in Bombay, set up an Iron foundry in 1852 and later on the developed cotton ginning and flour milling enterprise in the city.[49]

In 1857, N.C. Richardson opened the Byculla Iron and Metal Mart which was situated on Parel Road with branch works in Nesbit Road, Mazagaon.[50] Besides, East India Company's ordinance factory, established quite early in the beginning of the nineteenth century, employed nearly 1000 workers in its gun carriage section in 1823[51] and cotton bale screwing and spressing firms which started in the early eighteenth century, developed so many in number and so large in size that by the middle of the nineteenth century one of them employed 1000 persons.[52]

By this time, Western India also witnessed the birth of what may be called the nascent economic nationalism which was voiced by section of the first crop of the Elphinston Institution. Bhasker Pandurang Tarkhadkar, younger brother of Dadoba Pandurang Tarkhadkar, interalia criticized British economic policy in India and declared: "The whole wealth of India was now being transported to Great Britain and we have no employment left to us. You will perhaps say that it is our duty that we should do everything in our power to ameliorate the condition of our fellow countrymen which is fair enough and we admit the truth of it, but every project that we form to ourselves for such an undertaking would require a capital far beyond our reach to realize. You have taken away our money and how could we be able to shift for ourselves. You have made us wholly dependent which is all impossible."[53] While continuing his letters, he charged the British to have reduced 'India's sons and daughters to beggary' and further remarked that "The days are past when the natives were rolling in all the splendor of eastern grandeur which to this day has been proverbial among you, and the days too are passed when you could boast of nothing but a skin for clothing and a few animals for your food." In 1840, Gopal Hari Deshmukh *alias* 'Lokhitwadi' wrote *'Shatpatre'*, a hundred letters published in the *Prabhakar*,[54] a Marathi newspaper of Bombay, established by Govind Vithal Kunte alias Bhau Mahajan in 1840. In these letters, Deshmukh severely criticized the Brahmins and declared the British Rule highly beneficial; but he also expressed his disapproval of British Economic Policies which were impoverishing the people of India. This was further development of the ideas of economic nationalism which somewhat took concrete shape when Dr. Bhau Daji mooted in 1851 the proposal for textile mill in Bombay.[55] During the first half of the 1850s, the idea for a textile mill in Bombay took a concrete shape, preparing ground for the next stage of economic nationalism.

During the second half of the 19th century, British capital got very firmly rooted in Bombay. The raw materials exported to Great Britain were via Bombay and Calcutta. The only difference between the two cities was that Calcutta exported mainly Jute while Bombay became the exporter of cotton. As a result of this Calcutta became the chief centre of Jute industry while Bombay developed the cotton industry. The another point of difference in both the cities was that the Calcutta was directly developed by the British Firms as a result of colonial exploitation while Bombay came to be developed by means of independent native capital which too was indirectly an instance of colonial exploitation. Consequently, independent capitalist development took place relatively late in Calcutta than Bombay where the resistance of freedom loving Marathas forced the colonialists to grant the native wealthy classes greater independence and more favorable terms for their collaboration. Thus, Bombay developed as the sector of national capitalist economy under the most favorable conditions possible in colonial India. It was this favorable conditions that existed for the collaboration with British capital and became chiefly responsible for the building up of cotton mills by the Parsi-Gujarati big merchants of Bombay in collaboration with the British Capitalists. As a result of this development, the first group of the national capitalists emerged in the personalities like Dadabhoy Nawroji, Ferozshah Mehta and M.G. Ranade. Thus, the heroic resistance by the Marathas against colonialists benefited the natives in two ways. *Firstly,* it enriched the patriotic traditions of the people and, *secondly,* it also led to the appearance of the conditions in which new classes of Indian Society emerged.

In the year 1919, the Indian Industrial Commission reported that most of the capital invested in the cotton mills of Bombay consisted of profits derived from the opium export to China and the commission attributed to the gains which the cotton boom brought to Bombay in the 1860s.[56] The capital required for the building of textile mills was acquired from the trade in opium, cotton and British textiles while acting in collaboration with the English capitalists. Thus, was laid the foundation for the *factory industry* in India by the emerging capitalists of Bombay. It should be borne in mind that the British capitalists began to construct Jute mills at Calcutta two years later. This fact is a clear proof that the Bombay merchants were better prepared to undertake industrial ventures than other groups of Indian traders elsewhere and they did not refrain from investing their capital into large scale industry rather than to invest in the commercial and money lending fields. The Bombay merchants could take up the industrial ventures because they had well learnt from their collaboration with the English capitalists about the risks involved in the capital investment in the modern industry. This has induced some scholars to point out the comprador status of Parsi-Gujarati capitalists in Bombay[57].

The commercial relations which the merchants of Bombay maintained with the cotton growing areas of India and with overseas market *i.e.*, Middle East and China, contributed to the fact that the first Indian mill-owners arose from their ranks. As far back as 18th century, Bombay merchants acting as middlemen helped to sell British commodities in their markets, especially in China. The marketing of British yarn in China acquired great importance in the middle of the 19th century. It was precisely this trade in yarn which suggested the idea to the Bombay merchants for building spinning mills. An economist, T.R. Sharma wrote that "Some of these Parsi merchants realized that Bombay itself could provide a very good venue for the manufacture of yarn from the Indian cotton for export to the China market. The import of coal from England solved the problem of power and the first cotton mill in Bombay was started by Cawasji Nanabhoy Davar in 1851 and by 1860, some more mills were added. Thus, the early cotton mill industry of Bombay was not started to serve the home market but was rather intended to supply yarn to the overseas foreign markets in China and the Far East." [58]

That was the reason why upto the 19th century the output of yarn in the mills of Bombay far surpassed the production of cloth, although a part of the later was also exported. The orientation of the cotton mills of Bombay towards the overseas market was obviously forced upon them by the circumstance that the weak native industry was as yet unable to compete with the British textiles which were already firmly established in the Indian market.

The industrial activity of the rich citizens of Bombay appeared, therefore, during its first stage to be simply the continuation of their collaboration with the foreigners. This had included assistance in the sale of British yarn in China. The building of factories by Indian capitalists made the representatives of Manchester to demand in the British Parliament for the imposition of an excise duty on Indian cloth equal to the custom duties that were levied on British textiles imported into India. They contended that it was this custom duty that created favourable conditions for the building of cotton mills in Bombay. Hence they were afraid that the creation of industry would obstruct the exploitation of India as an agricultural country.

As stated above, the first company for the building of a cotton spinning mill in Bombay was set up in 1851. It started working on Feb. 5, 1854 and its equipment were supplied by a British firm, *'Platt Brothers And Company of Oldham'* which became the principal supplier of machinery for the factories built later in Bombay.[59]

There is no information available regarding the composition of the Board of Directors in charge of the first factory built in Bombay. It is known that a Parsi merchant Cawasji Nanabhoy Davar was the promoter of the Company who was not a very rich merchant, because his name does not appear in the list of Bombay merchants who owned mills.[60] But the same Cawasji Nanabhoy Davar was able to open another spinning mill in 1857. After 1857, Davar's name is no longer mentioned.

The first weaving mill of Bombay, the Oriental began to operate in 1860. A few months later its shares were already quoted at 38 percent above par value. The productive capacity of the Oriental comprised fifty thousand spindles and one thousand looms. A joint stock company was set up to run this enterprise which was very large for those firms. Its Managing Board consisted of the biggest commercial magnates of Bombay and two British capitalists. The chairman of the Board of Directors was Cursetji N. Cama who came from an old family of merchants. According to R. P. Masani C. N. Cama was a close friend of Dadabhoy Nawroji. In 1855, when Cama's firm opened a branch in London, it became the first commercial company with an office of its own in Great Britain. Nawroji was appointed to represent Cama in London.[61] But relations were strained between the two friends in 1858 due to the fact that Nawroji did not like the opium and liquor trade carried on by the firm of Camas.[62] The opium was sold in China, while the liquor was imported from Europe into India. This was the reason why Cama maintained commercial relations with British and Chinese ports. In 1859 Nawroji started his own firm in London which traded in cotton and acted as broker.[63]

A son of a big merchant capitalist Jamshetji Jijibhoy, named Byramji Jijibhoy was a member of the Board of Directors and also became the Director of a number of other cotton mills. One of the other richest Parsi merchants of Bombay named Maneckji Petit was also the Director of Oriental Mill. He was engaged in commerce from the age of eighteen onwards and for commercial purposes he sailed to the shores of Arabia. Later on he became more stable in profit as well as in position when he served British firms in Bombay as a broker.[64] Petit's commercial transactions assumed such a large proportion that he became the owner of the large merchant vessel Charles Grant, with a displacement of 2000 tons which was rather large for those days. The regular trips were made by this vessel between India and China. Among the other Directors of the mill was a Hindu, Varjeevan Das Madhow Das, who hailed from the Kapol Bania community and who honestly served the financial interests of the British and, therefore, occupied the post of the Director of the Bank of Bombay, which indeed was an honor to a Bombay man. A Parsi Merwanji Framji Pandey, who acted as a broker to three British firms in Bombay, was a large shareholder and general manager of the 'Oriental Mill'.

It would be worth mentioning here of a Baghdadi Jew businessman who made Bombay his home in the year 1832. He began his career with a borrowed capital of one thousand pounds and built an empire worth billions. This Jew was no other than David Sassoon who was the descendent of the Biblical King David of Israel. His ancestors had risen to great prominence and acquired riches in Baghdad until misfortune fell upon his father named Sheikh Sassoon. Thereafter David Sassoon made up his mind and moved to Bombay where in 1832, he set up a business firm and started his commercial and financial transactions. Four years later he became a member of the Board of Administration of the Bombay Chamber of Commerce that had been established in 1836. In those days as a rule only representatives of British firms were admitted to the Board apart from David Sassoon. The only other native member of the Board of Administration in 1836 was Dadabhoy Pestonji.[65] From a small house in Tamarind Lane which served as a godown as well as office with the upper storey serving as living quarters; Sassoon began his import-export trade with Persia. He slowly began to buy wharfs and godowns along the sea front as and when he had money. With the increase of his international trade increased his assets too. As a true businessman Sassoon saw the possibility of immense growth in cotton trade and began to export cotton bales to England and import piece goods from there to be sold in Baghdad, Bushara and India. When trade with China opened, he set up branches at Canton, Hongkong and Sanghai. The Bombay office was looked after by his first son Albert while China trade was handled by his second son Elias who made Sanghai his headquarter and traded in opium, textile and silk. Elias was the first one to establish a branch at Yokohama, after the opening up of Japan. As Sassoon's eastern trade soared, his third son named Sassoon David, opened a branch in London Hall Street and began to prosper. The entire business of Sassoon was such a successful venture that David Sassoon became a multimillionaire and a leading businessman of

Bombay. Jamsetji Jijibhoy and Premchand Roychand were his contemporaries.

Inspite of his firm's business in Great Britain and in the Far East, Sassoon conducted their activities in India also. In the 1860s David Sassoon built docks for the repair of ships in Colaba in Bombay. The Sassoon owned factories for the processing of cotton and raw silk in Bombay. They also participated in the building of industrial enterprises. The Sassoons were known as the Rothschild of the East. As their biographer notes: "Silver and gold, silks, gums and spices, opium and cotton, wool and wheat-whatever more... bear the mark of Sassoon. Eventually, the family went to control the largest spinning and weaving power in the country."[66]

Other than the *'Oriental'*, six other factories started operating in 1860. The spinning mill *'Victoria'* and the weaving mill *'Maneckji Petit'* were started by Dinshaw Petit, the son of Maneckji N. Petit. Although Dinshaw Petit was the biggest manufacturer in Bombay he did not give up the commercial dealings which he inherited from his father. He was the only Indian Director of the Bank of the Presidency of Bombay. The businessmen of Bombay kept combined their industrial activities with the commercial transactions in collaboration with the British capitalists.

Some members of the Bhatia community also ventured into the industrial enterprises. Keshowji Naik started a weaving mill Royal. He was a broker to a British firm and a cotton merchant who became manufacturer. Another weaving mill *'Great Eastern'* was set up by a company headed by B. Jijibhoy, Khatau Makanji and Morarji Gokuldas who were the Bhatia merchants. Morarji Gokuldas began his career as an associate in the firm of his uncles, who were selling British textiles. The cotton mill *'Coorla'* was opened in the year 1860 itself by a Parsi named Bomanji H. Wadia. He belonged to the family of shipbuilders. A member of the Kapol Bania caste named Nathubhai Mangaldas started operating the sixth enterprise in 1860 who was the head of the Hindu community of Bombay.[67]

Nine factories were operating in Bombay by the end of

1860, six of which had been built in 1860 itself. It appeared as if Bombay was going to be just like Manchester but the Civil War of America in 1861 totally altered the situation. The Northern States of America blocked the supply of cotton to Great Britain, as a result of which the prices of Indian cotton got quadrupled, rising from Rs. 139 per Kandi in 1861 to Rs. 585 in 1864.[68] Consequently, the native merchants of Bombay started speculative business and therefore the capital that should have been utilized in industrial sectors came to be diverted towards making profit through the cotton boom. As a result of this the process of building factories came to be delayed and in place of that the joint stock companies, banks, finance corporations came to be floated with a view to invest more in cotton for getting more and quick profits.[69] In other words, the high prices of cotton led to its export rather than to feed the local industry which needed cheap cotton. Thus, there followed a slack period in growth and development of textile industries.

However, the end of the Civil War and the restoration of cotton supply by America to England once again changed the business scenario for the native merchants who came to be ruined in thousands. It was at this time that the Bank of Bombay got crushed. Inspite of this, the businessmen of Bombay managed to make a profit of Rs. 60 to 70 crores out of the cotton boom.[70]

The big businessmen who collaborated with the British grew rich through the cotton trade. Many traders of average means also made fortune during this period. Some of these merchants became the promoters and managers of new companies but more often they were just ordinary shareholders. A certain amount of pressure was also exerted by mill owners, when signing contracts, for future deliveries, cotton suppliers had to promise that they would acquire a number of shares.

The cotton fever forced the colonial authorities to introduce a tariff scale for railway transport with the aim of encouraging the export of cotton. The new tariff also lowered the charges made for the delivery of cotton to the mills situated in Bombay, which became the most important railway junction in Western India in 1870s. The transport of finished cloth from Bombay to the inland markets became considerably cheaper, because for the benefit of the British importers, the railway reduced freight charges for the carriage of textiles from the ports to the interior of the country. The policy which the colonial authorities pursued with regard to railway freight charges led to the concentration of the cotton industry in Bombay, which is comparatively distant from both the cotton growing regions and the main markets.

The second group of Bombay Industrialists arose from the rank of cotton dealers who were the byproduct of the cotton boom that led to enhanced cotton trade. Among the big capitalists who played a very active role in the industrial programme of sixtees was the Parsi P. R. Kolah and the first Muslim mill-owner, Kasumbhai Dharmsey was a Gujarati Khoja Muslim and a trader. Both these persons were well known cotton merchants. Kasumbhai Dharmsey continued conducting large scale commercial transactions in collaboration with the British even after becoming a mill owner and was considered to be one of the richest man in India.[71] P. R. Kolah was a business partner of Dadabhoy Nawroji.[72]

Among the Indian capitalists of the later half of the 19th century, the most prominent personality was of Jamshetji Nusserwanji Tata, a Parsi. His father Nusserwanji Tata was the first to break away from his family profession of priestly functions for the sake of doing business. When he arrived in Bombay, he had no money as has been informed by a relative of the Tatas and one of the managers of Tata concern named N. Saklatvala.[73] Jamshedji Nusserwanji Tata acquired good fortune by supplying war materials to British during their war with Iran in 1857 after which he became independent and started his commercial transactions with China. Together with his partner, who was a Hindu named Kalyan Das; J. N. Tata established his firm *'Nusserwanji and Kalyan Das'* in December 1859 in Hongkong. This firm imported opium and cotton into

China and exported tea, silk, camphor, copper and gold from China.

During the period of cotton boom, *'Nusservanji and Kalyan Das'* firm also started speculative business in cotton but as was the fate of other traders and merchants, the sudden stoppage of Civil War brought the firm on the verge of total bankruptcy but credit goes to the boldness and honesty of Jamshedji Nassurwanji Tata that he not only settled with his creditors but was also successful in re-establishing his firm very soon. It was during this boom period that he was sent to Manchester for concluding agreements for the supply of cotton and there he saw the most up-to-date machinery for setting up the industry. However, the real opportunity to make good money came his way in 1867, when along with few other Bombay traders Jamshedji Nassurwanji Tata started war supplies during British march against Ethiopia.[74]

After two more years, J. N. Tata began his industrial career in 1869 when he built-up the cotton mill *'Alexandra'* in Bombay. This cotton mill yielded him a very high return but this enterprising man was not satisfied with rather small mill, and concluded that if more profits were to be made then such mills were to be set up at a place into interior where labour power could be obtained at a cheaper rates, cotton could be procured easily and the market be very near rendering easy and cheap transportation. Therefore, he sold the Alexandra mill to Keshowji Naik in 1871 and himself chose Nagpur as a convenient place for building a new mill. The new mill called *'Empress'* started operating from January 1877. Its name was kept in honour of Queen Victoria of Great Britain. It was in this mill that he tried all his ways of exploiting the worker's labour power by introducing a premium system for uninterrupted attendance at work and for length of service, to induce the exhausted workers to continue the backbreaking toil in the mill for as long as possible. There was also a worker's joint stock company with a capital of Rs. 50,000/- which issued shares of ten rupees carrying a dividend of 4 percent to utilize even the pitiful savings of the workers.[75]

The Empress Mill yielded a very high return of profit to J. N. Tata, so much so that the dividends paid by the mill reached 16 percent as early as 1881. The average dividends for the first twenty years were 20 percent, while the average annual profit yielded was 40 percent which included deductions made for the reserve fund of the enterprise. By 1920, the total returns of the Empress Mill amounted to Rs. 75,000,000 *i.e.*, 50 times the capital initially invested. Between 1877 and 1907 the capital of the company grew from Rs. 1, 5000,000 to Rs. 4,700,000 over a period of 43 years of its operation.[76] Thus, the enormous profit acquired by J. N. Tata through the exploitation of workers led to the vast accumulation of capital which later came to be invested in the building of Iron and steel works and a hydro-electric power station.

Other than Tata, the members of Bhatia community, who earlier worked as collaborators of British started building factories. The name of M. Gokuldas and Sunderlal Jaitha is worth mentioning in this respect. The later was a biggest cotton merchant and the owner of ships. He also owned many enterprises for cleaning and pressing cotton in Maharashtra. The credit goes to Sunderlal Jaitha for building three mills, one after another, out of which one was opened in Bombay in the year 1872, the other one in Madras in 1874 and the third one in Jalgaon in Maharashtra in the year 1872. Another member of the Bhatia Community and a cotton merchant named Thakersey Moolji also became a manufacturer in 1873.

Although after the cotton boom, the new mill owners emerged mainly from amongst the cotton merchants, who collaborated with the British capitalists, but it would not be proper to maintain that these capitalists were only from the ranks of merchants trading in cotton. Those merchants who acted as middlemen in other commercial activities also became the manufacturers.

In 1874, eleven new mills came to be started in Bombay. The Petits started two mills in this year and became the biggest textile manufacturer in India. The Sassoon who had risen to fame on account of their cotton trade during the boom period also started a cotton mill. Among the other capitalists who opened mills in 1874 were Ahmed Habibbhoy, B. R. Mody and Ardeshir H. Wadia.

Ahmed Habibbhoy was one of the two Indian Directors of the Bank of Bombay. This indicates that he was closely associated with British capital. A Parsi named Burjorji R. Mody began to build his mill as soon as he returned from China where he represented the Tata enterprises. Ardeshir H. Wadia belonged to the family of shipbuilders and was a contractor of East India Company.

If the enterprises of Sassoon is not considered than also the British capital started operating its first cotton mill in 1874. The British capitalists had their interests in the cotton industry of Bombay even much earlier. This is proved by the example that two British dealers were the members of the Board of Administration of the *Oriental Mill,* But it was only in 1874 that an Englishman became the Managing Director of a cotton mill in Bombay for the first time. This man was James Dunkerley, an agent of a British firm which supplied machinery for mills built in Bombay. Many British ship owners in Bombay went there originally as representatives of British machine building firms and then became rich. The Indian Textile Journal wrote later in February 1928 that the founders of the mills in Bombay were local cotton traders and bankers who were helped by the owners of engineering works in Lancashire, and by merchants and craftsman sent to India by the factory owners. A few years later, they were joined by several building firms and successful factory managers. Some of those who set up factories of their own were interested in the sale of machinery, for they were agents of British engineering firms which manufactured thereon. All these founders worked jointly on the Board of Directors which had a rather cosmopolitan membership. The actual leadership however, was in the hands of managing agencies. Certain firms or families by right of succession almost always held there managing agencies.

The fact that the agents of machine building enterprises became mill owners indicates that the developing large scale industry in India was completely dependent on Britain for the supply of machinery for the factories. The colonial regime, which delayed the industrial development of India, obstructed the creation of machine building industry in India. This strengthened dependence of Indian industrialists on British capital, forcing them to 'collaborate' with the later on unfavourable terms.

The dependence of the Indian industry on the supply of machinery from Great Britain determined to a great extent the methods used by British capital to penetrate it. The British suppliers of machinery granted Indian capitalists who were building factories, deferred payment terms for the machinery they purchased. Only a third of the price was usually paid in cash. A high rate of interest approximately 6% was charged for the remaining amount, until it was completely paid off. If delays occurred in the payment of the debt, the British supplier of the machinery became joint owners of the enterprise. Using their monopoly position in respect of the supply of machinery, they not only forced the manufacturers in Bombay to give them a share in the profit, but seized direct control of the large scale industry through their agents, who became Managers and Directors. Outwardly this often looks as the form of co-operation of British and Indian capitalists, in one and the same company and the 'fusion' of their capitals. But in reality the Indian 'Partners' did by no means enjoy equal rights.

The British machine-building companies were represented by their commercial agents in the industry of Bombay. The building of mills enabled these agents to make good money. The agents usually charged a commission of 5% on the value of the machinery they sold. Since the machinery of one mill cost from Rs. 7,00,000 to Rs. 8,00,000 the agent could earn upto Rs. 50,000 during the building of one enterprise, if the inevitable additional receipts such as bribes and premium are taken into account. Frequently the agents invested the money they accumulated in the building of new enterprises. By this means, moreover, they eliminated the competition of other British supplier of machinery, for the agents, who became shareholders and could influence the business of the company.

After the mill was put into operation, the agents usually sold their shares. They invested money thus realized in another mill about to be built, thereby making sure of receiving the new orders for the supply of machinery.

However, these earnings could not provide sufficient funds for the venture. In 1883, for instance, the firm of the former agents George Cotton and John Greaves started five cotton mills in Bombay. Greaves and Cotton could not have managed to do this without the help from Great Britain. This aid was not confined to purely financial assistance. The fact that these manufacturers were members of the British capitalists class which ruled India, gave them a real advantage over the Indian managing agents. By relying upon their dominating position in the economy and the state apparatus, the British managing agents could mobilize and place under their control the investments of numerous Indian shareholders. The greater part of the ordinary share capital of British Industrial companies usually belonged to Indian shareholders. The British managing agents received not only their portion of the super profits but, in the shape of founder's shares, premiums, commissions and other deductions, appropriated that part of the super profits which should have accrued to the capital of their Indian partners. The rate of profit obtained by the British managing agents was usually considerably higher than the rate of dividends of the Indian shareholders. The Indian stock-holders who owned ordinary shares, therefore, had to be satisfied with dividends corresponding approximately to the average rate of profit obtained on industrial capital, which was however considerably lower than the actual colonial rate of surplus value extracted at the given enterprise. Indian capitalists thus helped the British companies which were acting as managing agencies to extract huge profits by exploiting the workers and peasantry of India. At the same time, such a partition of profit gave rise to serious contradictions between British capital and Indian capitalists which was dependent on it.

The industrial activity got revived to some extent in 1874 after which a slack period followed till 1882. Between 1874 to 1882, only two industrial enterprises were built in Bombay. The factory owners were the Hindu Premchand Roychand and

Manmohandas Ramji. Premchand Roychand was the biggest speculator in landed property and a partner of Tata while Manmohandas Ramji traded in British textiles and represented the Ralli Brothers, the leading cotton export company.[77]

The year 1883 witnessed the birth of as many as thirteen mills in Bombay which became a record in the history of the cotton industry. Five of these mills were owned by the British firm, Greaves, Cotton and Co., while three other mills came to be founded by other British companies including Sassoon. Thus in 1883 the British capital made its entry in the cotton industry of Bombay.

The new mills also came to be built by the big businessmen of Bombay like Dinshaw M. Petit, N. B. Jijibhoy and a few other merchants. The name of a Parsi named Kaikhusro Heera Manek is worth mentioning in this respect. In 1883 he started a weaving mill 'The Queen' and in 1882 two spinning mills. He began his career as a cashier of the Bombay Baroda Railway Line and in 1868 he became a broker on the stock exchange. In 1880 he began to trade in cotton and built several cotton pressing establishments. The favourable economic situation of the eightees gave Heera Manek the opportunity to become quickly-rich. But after his death in 1893, the company he had established could not withstand the difficulties which arose at the turn of the century and was ruined. In general it can he concluded that the attempts of the small capitalists of Bombay to established independent industrial enterprises inevitably ended in failure.

In 1884, Nusserwanji Ardashir Wadia, another member of the family of former shipbuilder, opened his first industrial enterprise. His firm *'N. Wadia and sons'* acted as agent for four British engineering works which specialized in textile machinery. This firm fitted out fourteen mills in Bombay alone. Two more native brokers dealing in machinery built cotton mills in 1896. They were Nawroji Wadia, the son of Nusserwanji Wadia and Shapur Sorabji, the grandson of the gunsmith and contractor of the East India Company. Nawroji Wadia received his education in Liverpool and was perhaps the first Indian to become a trained engineer. After his return to Bombay in 1866 he worked as manager in the factories of Petit. In 1878, he opened a firm for the supply of machinery, which was connected with four British companies manufacturing textile machinery. Shapur Sorabji received higher technical education in Great Britain and gained practical experience in British factories. Before his return to India, in 1887 Sorabji was presented to Queen Victoria by the Secretary of State for India. At that time, Indians trained as engineers were very rare and did not endanger the monopoly of the British specialists.

Incidentally, only very few Indian engineers graduated during the following decades. The Victoria Jubilee Technical Institute, which was opened in Bombay in April 1889, trained only skilled mechanics. Although the capitalists of Bombay had spent much on this institution, they did not obtain Indian engineers for their factories.[78]

Thus, there existed in Bombay two types of firms that supplied machinery for the building up of factories. One of these was of British firms while the other was a group of Indians which were dependent upon the British supplier. A notable point in this connection is that the British firms maintained a considerably higher interest of profits than the Indian firms. The Greaves, Cottons and later Brady's and Bradbury's could build industrial enterprises so quickly and on such a large scale. This was due to the fact that the capitalists of Bombay had to hand over a large portion of their profits to the representatives of British capital. The only Indian agents for the supply of machinery who gradually became big manufacturer were the Wadias, but it took them several decades.

Upto the end of the 19th century, the pace of industrial development was very rapid in Bombay. By 1891 sixty seven cotton mills operated in the town.[79] At the close of the 19th century British capital continued to strengthen its position in the development and growth of industry of Bombay. In 1895 and 1896, the Sassoon built two more mills and became the biggest mill owners in the cotton industry of India. The biggest firm in India for the import of textile, Killick, Nixon and Co. opened its first enterprise in 1896.[80] This British firm combined the manufacture of cloth in India with the import of cloth from Great Britain.

Of the 57 new enterprises started in Bombay during the period from 1881 to 1990, British capitalists, including Sassoon built 18 mills. The participation of British capital in the building of industrial enterprises in Bombay reached its peak during this period. By 1895, fourteen of the seventy mills operating in Bombay were directly controlled by British capitalists.[81]

At the close of the 19th century, the merchants who collaborated with the British and formed the top strata of Bombay merchant continued to strengthen their position in the textile industry of the town. In 1888, Ebrahim Currimbhoy, the founder of the richest 'dynasty' of Muslim manufacturers, put his first spinning mill into operation. Currimbhoy was a member of the Khoja Muslim community, a Gujarati trading caste. He began his business career by setting up a firm in Hongkong. Afterward, he opened offices in Calcutta, Singapore, Shanghai and Kobe in Japan. The commodities which this big merchant handled included opium, cotton and yarn which he exported to the Far East, and tea which he imported from China. Currimbhoy built a number of enterprises in Maharashtra and Indore for the initial processing of the cotton he exported.

The cotton industry occupied prominent place in the economy of Bombay despite the closer of several mills in the early nineties. In the Cotton Mills of Bombay were employed 102 thousand workers and in the other branches of large scale industry there were 33 thousand workers in 1908. Side by side with the machine industry, several tens of thousands of handicraftsmen were engaged in some branches of small scale industry. In addition to the mills, whose products were sold not in India but also in the countries of the near and Far East, there were small weaving shops which manufactured local varieties of clothes to satisfy the needs of the different sections of the population in Bombay. In 1901, there were 7,500 weavers, in other branches of production like shoemakers, potters, jewelers, tobacco workers, butter and oil manufacturers, confectioners and bakers catered for the requirements of the half million inhabitants of the town.

In the second half of the 19th century, Bombay continued to develop as major centre through which the commerce between Great Britain and India was carried on. By 1890s, the total turnover of Bombay's foreign trade had increased eleven times more than it was in the forties. Among the imported commodities cloth and yarn occupied the first place, making up 40% to 50% of the total value of the imports. It was followed by liquor which made up approximately 20%, and sugar approximately 10% of the total. Therefore, a far greater part of the import trade consisted either of consumer goods which by the end of the 19th century India could have already produced by modern Industrial methods or of alcoholic drinks which were mainly consumed by British officials, officers and soldiers. But the beginning of the import of British capital and the building of industrial enterprises by Indian capital led to the appearance of a new import item-machinery-which was still small but steadily growing. At the end of the 19th century, it amounted only to 5% of the total value of the commodities, imported into Bombay. Each machine that was imported into India increased the extent of the contradictions that would arise in the future between imperialist Britain and colonial India.

From the 1850s onwards, cotton supplanted opium as the principal commodity exported from Bombay. By the close of 19th century it made up one-third of the total value of exports. Next came oil seeds and wheat. The volume of the opium export increased upto the seventies and only then began its gradual decline. Even at the close of the 19th century Rs. 30 million worth of opium was annually exported from Bombay to Asian countries. Thus, the export consisted chiefly of the type of commodities that are characteristics of a source of agricultural raw materials. But the composition of the export trade too was changed by the growth of industrial production and in the last decade of the 19th century yarn and cloth amounted to over a quarter of the total value of the commodities exported from Bombay.[82]

The merchants of Bombay continued to participate actively in the foreign commerce of their town, although sea faring by Indians was greatly restricted by the almost complete monopoly of sea-transport. The Parsis transported goods to China, Japan and even Europe. The Indian and Muslim merchants carried on a lively trade with the countries of the near East and the British colonies in Eastern Africa.[83]

The semi-government Bank of Bombay and the British Exchange banks occupied a dominant position in the financial sphere both in Bombay and other towns. The financial organization was still in the early stage of development. There were no indigenous joint stock banks and the merchants and the manufactures used their individual connections and relied on the trading and credit relations that existed within the caste organizations to obtain loans, especially long terms loans. The leading figure in this financial system was the indigenous banker, or Shroff, who represented big money lending and loan capital. The Marwari money lenders played a very important role in the credit system of Bombay. About this community much has been stated in one of the earlier chapter. Here it would be sufficient to state that the members of this community were the immigrants from Rajasthan who worked in Bombay as moneylenders to speculators in opium, cotton, silver and gold. By the early years of 20th century Marwari money lending capital got firmly established in Bombay and the Marwari moneylenders spread their net among all sections of the population of Bombay. They found their clients in all walks of life, from the heir apparent to the mill hands.[84]

At the beginning of the 20th century, the big Indian capitalist of Bombay were mainly comprised of Gujaratis although there was also a strong group of Marwari capitalist that had began to emerge. Commerce in Bombay remained to a considerable extent in the hands of people who spoke

Gujarati and the local traders as per the Gazetteer of Bombay City and Island.

However, the Gujarati merchants of Bombay did not monopolize the trade of the city. Bombay was considered a rich town and as W. Digby wrote, a sufficient large amount of capital circulated there to satisfy all the requirements of this great port. Where did this capital come from? The greater part belonged to foreigners, to European mercantile banks and European merchants (other than English). The bulk of the indigenous capital did not come from local sources but belonged to Indian bankers and merchants from the native principalities who owned approximately Rs. 60 million of the capital that circulated in Bombay. An important group of rich merchants who had more or less settled down in Bombay were, moreover, emigrants from the native states.[85] The majority of these capitalists were local bankers and merchants from the Gujarati principalities of Kathiawar and Baroda. But among them were, undoubtedly Marwari, Hindustani and other non-Gujarati merchants. The non-Gujarati capitalists played more important part in the commerce of Bombay than in its industry, where the families of hereditary Bombay merchants predominated. It can be maintained that the indigenous merchants of Bombay were induced to invest their accumulation by merchants coming from the interior.

According to the Gazetteer of Bombay City and Island (Vol. 1), the capitalists of Bombay belonged to the Gujarati caste and communities *i.e.*, Bhatia's, Banias, Bohras, Khojas, Memons, Jews and Parsis in addition to Marwari's. "The Bhatia's are chiefly cloth merchants, landlords and mill owners, the Jains of Gujarat are bankers, jewelers, Shroffs and commission agents, while those of Cutch are grain merchants and cotton brokers. The Marwari's are money lenders and speculate in opium, cotton, silver and gold, the Banias do the same and are traders of every denominations. The Khojas are landlords, mill owners, general merchants, contractors, and do a large trade in imports and exports. The Bohras and Memons are landlords, contractors, stationary merchants and general traders and do a large trade in imports and exports. The Parsis are ubiquitous in every branch of trade. The European capitalist is usually a large importer and exporter."[86]

The only Maratha caste mentioned is the Brahmins from the Deccan, listed among the castes that have produced some of the wealthy inhabitants of Bombay. Since there were no businessmen among the Brahmins at that time one can assume that the, wealthy Marathas were either landowners who lived in Bombay or prosperous members of the free professions, in the main, that of lawyers. The following table shows the number of mills built by the different religious communities of Bombay during the period 1854 to 1900.[87]

Years	*No. of Mills built*	*Number of mills built by*				
		Parsis	*Hindus*	*Muslims*	*Total Indians*	*British including sassoon*
1854-1870	13	9	3	1	13	—
1871-1880	17	4	8	2	14	3
1881-1890	39	17	6	3	26	13
1891-1900	18	6	4	3	13	5
Total	87	36	21	9	66	21

The above mentiones Table given by S. M. Rutnagur clearly brings out that three quarter of the cotton industry was built by the Indian capitalists. The Parsi capitalist played a leading role in setting up cotton mills in Bombay. Next to them came the Hindu capitalists. During the first sixteen years, *i.e.*, 1854 to 1870, the Parsis built nine mills while the members of other communities built only four mills. Perhaps this was due to the fact that Parsis were engaged in the commercial business that had enabled them to have the accumulated capital for investment in cotton industry. Except between 1871 to 1880, the Parsis built the mills more than other communities till 1900. It was only between this decade (1871-1880) that the Hindus managed to built eight mills, while Parsis built four and Muslims two mills. It also follows from the above table that the Muslims community, which also collaborated with the British, was slow in the investment of their capital in the industry of Bombay till the close of the 19th century.

The another Table reproduced by S. M Rutnagur gives the more interesting data regarding the actual number of mills controlled by Indian capitalists, community wise, and by the British.[88]

Control of Cotton Mills in Bombay

	1895		1915	
Religion	*Firms*	*Mills*	*Firms*	*Mills*
Hindu	27	30	11	18
Parsi	15	22	14	25
Muslim	04	04	07	11
Total controlled by Indians	46	56	32	54
British Including Sassoons	04	14	08	29
Grand Total	50	70	40	83

The above table indicates that by 1895, the Indian capitalists controlled 56 mills and 46 firms while the mills came down to 54 and the firms to 32 by 1915. At the same time, number of mills controlled by British was 14 in 1895 which increased to 29 by 1915. It implies that the British capital surpassed the Indians capital by the opening decade of the 20th century. This could be because of the closing down of some mills or due to their amalgamation with other mills. The another fact that emerges from the above table is that Hindu capitalists who controlled a large number of mills by the close of the 19th century had to resign their leading position to the Parsi manufacturers in the 20th century.

One of the chief characteristics of the Bombay industrial capitalists was that they carried on commercial transactions on a large scale as intermediaries of foreigners. In fact all Bombay manufacturers happened to be chiefly the merchants. The Bhatia and Khoja capitalists were big land-owners while the Parsis were the richest owners of landed property in Bombay. However, landed property was not the principal object of the business activities of the capitalists of Bombay.

At the close of the 19th century and in the early 20th century, important changes took place in the cotton industry of Bombay. Earlier Bombay cotton industry worked for the foreign market, especially China, but from the early 20th century it turned towards the home market. This industry was designed for the export of yarn to China hence the output of fabrics for the home market always remained smaller. In the latter half of the 19th century, the export of yarn from Bombay to China grew rapidly. It rose from 19,817 bales in 1876 to 77,000 bales in 1881 and 403 thousand in 1891. It reached its highest level in 1905 when it went to 651 thousand bales.[89] The importance of yarn production in Bombay can be understood from the fact that between 1910 and 1904 the average annual output of Bombay mills was approximately 800 thousand bales.[90] But from 1905 onwards, the export of yarn from Bombay decreased continuously, falling from 405 thousand bales in 1915 to 108 thousand in 1908 and a few tens of thousands of bales in the twenties.[91] This change in the export of cotton yarn occurred due to the fact that China and Japan set up their own machine industry for the manufacture of cotton yarns.

In the expanding home market, the Bombay manufacturers came across with difficulties on account of the increased competitions from the side of the British capitalists and also because the size of the home market was quite limited on account of the prevailing colonial conditions. It was this increased competition that broke off the *'cordial relations'* between the native capitalists and the European capitalists because their interests started clashing. The Indian National Congress Party, which saw its birth as a result of the combined efforts of Bombay capitalists and the colonial administrators, very soon turned to be hostile to British imperialists because of the native capitalist's opposition. The rise of this opposition was the result of the discriminatory policy, adopted by British administration at the instance of British capitalists, in the levying of the tariff duties. Excise duty was imposed on the cotton goods produced in India and import duty on British goods came to be reduced, as a result of which the Indian goods found it very difficult to compete in the market. The only solution to this could be the technical reorganization of machine industry with a view to increase the production of cloths and reduce the output of yarn for sale. Consequently, the number of weaving looms increased in Bombay. However the weak companies could not withstand the difficulties of reorganization and more than two third of the cotton industry of Bombay went bankrupt between the period 1895 to 1915. Even some firms belonging to big merchants, who collaborated with the British, failed as a result of reorientation towards the home market. The oldest enterprise of Bombay, the oriental mill was the first one to go bankrupt. It was taken over by Peerbhoy Adamji, a member of the Bohra community. Similarly the majority of enterprise that had become insolvent came to be taken over by the British firms Brady and Bradbury, Sassoon or by the stronger Indian companies owned by persons like Pettis, Currimbhoy, Gokuldas and Habibbhoy.

Thus, since the early 20th century the building of new mills in Bombay came to stagnation because the older companies preferred to acquire managing agencies, rather than to start new enterprises. This was so because, as Vera Anstey wrote: "It saved them from worries helped to increase the capital and reduced the risk."[92] Of the nine industrial enterprises built in Bombay upto 1914, two belonged to N. Wadia, a commission agent for the supply of machinery, and one each to Tata, Currimbhoy and James Finely and Co., a British firm specializing in the export of cotton.

The early 20th century was on the whole a period during which both British capital and the strong individual representatives of Indian merchant capital, who collaborated with the British, were consolidating their positions in the textile industry of Bombay.

REFERENCES

1. Max Weber: The Religion of India (Translated by Hans Gerth and don Martindale), p. 112.

2. *Ibid.*

3. *G.B.C.I.*, Vol. I, p. 249.

4. S D. Mehta: 'The Indian Cotton Textile Industry: 1854-1954' (Bombay, 1955), p. 22.

5. *Ibid.*

6. D. R. Gadgil: Notes on the Rise of Business Communities in India, Origins of the Modern Indian Business Class – An Interim Report (New York, 1957).

7. Ashok V. Desai: 'The Origins of Parsee Enterprise', The Indian Economic and Social History Review (Dec.1964), pp. 307-317.

8. Amiya Kumar Bagchi: 'European and Indian Entrepreneurship in India: 1900-1950' in E. Leach and S.N. Mukharjee (ed.) Elites in South Asia, Cambridge, England...)

9. V. I. Pavlov: Historical Premises for India's Transition to Capitalism (Moscow, 1979). The Indian Capitalist Class: A Historical Study (Bombay, 1964). V. I. Pavlov, L. I. Rensner and G. K. Shirkov: Indians Social and Economic Development: 18th – 20th Centuries (Moscow, 1975).

10. Eckchard Kulcke: The Parsis in India (Delhi, 1978).

11. Thomas A. Timberg: The Marwaris: From Traders to Industrialists (New Delhi, 1978).

12. Amlendu Guha: 'The Comprador Role of Parsi Sethia: 1750-1850.' Economic and Political, Weekly (November 28, 1970), pp. 1933-1936.

13. Milton Singer: *When a Great Tradition modernize An Anthropological Approach to Indian Civilization (New York, 1972)*, pp. 309-10.

14 Thomas A. Timberg : *Op.cit.*, p. 40.

15 R. S. Rungta: *The Rise of Business Corporations in India: 1851-1900' (Cambridge, 1970)* p. 40.

16 D. P. Pandit: *'Creative Response in Indian Economy: A Regional Analysis' in 'Economic Weekly, Bombay, IX (February 23 and March 2, 1957)*, pp. 283-285.

17 K.L. Gillion: *Ahmadabad: A Study in Urban History, (Berkley, Calif, 1964)* p. 81.

18 Hemlata Acharya: *'Creative Response in Indian Economy: A Comment', Economic Weekly, Bombay IX (April 17, 1957)*, pp. 547-549.

19. R.S. Rungta: *Op.cit.*, p. 165.

20. *Ibid.*

21. V. I. Pavlov: *Historical Premises for India's Transition to Capitalism, late 18th to mid. 19th Century (Moscow, 1979); The Indian Capitalist Class: A Historical Study (Bombay, 1964); V.I. Pavlov, L. I. Reisner, G. K. Shirkov: India's Social and Economic Development: 18th – 20th Century (Moscow, 1975).*

22. Amlendu Guha: *Op.cit.*, pp. 1932-36.

23. *Bombay Gazette, 11th July, 1854;* S. D. Mehta: *Op.cit.*, p. 15.

24. R.H. Jalbhoy: *The Portrait Gallery of Western India (Bombay, 1896).*

25. *Ibid.*

26. Dumasia: *A Short Biographical Sketch of Late Sheth Varjivan Das Madav Das*, p. 5.

27. *Ibid.*, p. 19.

28. W. H. Sleeman: *Rambels and Recollections of an Indian Official*, Vol. II, p. 143.

29. G. N. Madgaonkar: *Mumbaiche Varnan*, pp. 218-19.

30. *A Surat letter to Council Nov. 1676.*

31. *G. B. C. I.*, Vol. I, p. 462.

32. *Gazetteer of Bombay Presidency (Materials Towards...)* Vol. I, pp. 152-154.

33. *Ibid.*

34. *G. B. C. I.*, Vol. I, p. 389.

35. *Ibid.*, p. 390.

36. *Ibid.*

37. *Ibid.*

38. B. S. Rao: *Surveys of Indian Industries (O. U. P.; Madras, 1958)*, p. 35.

39. *Ibid.*

40. *Ibid.*, p. 34.

41. *Gazetteer of Bombay Presidency, (Material towards...)*, Vol. II, p. 326 in C. R. Low: *History of The Indian Navy*, Vol. I, pp. 540-41.

42. V. I. Pavlov: *Historical Premises for India's Transition To Capitalism*, p. 322.

43. H.A. Young: *East India Company's Arsenal (Oxford, 1937)*, pp. 73-74.

44. *G. B. C.I.*, Vol. I, pp. 475-76.

45. *Ibid.* p. 469.

46. *Ibid.*

47. *Ibid.*, p. 470.

48. *Ibid.*

49. S. M. Rutnagur: *Bombay Industries, The Cotton Mills*; p. 726.

50. *G.B.C.I.*, Vol. I, p. 500.

51. S. M. Young: *The East India Company's Arsenal*, p. 202.

52. *The Bombay Times, Calender of 1855*, p. 99.

53. *Bombay Gazetteer, August 20, 1841 (Letter of Hindoo).*

54. Nalini Pandit: *Maharashtrateel Rashtravadacha Vikas*, p. 19.

55. S. D. Mehta: *Indian Cotton Textile Industry (1854-1954)*, p. 7.

56. *Indian Industrial Commission, A Report (London, 1919), I, p. 65.*

57. Amlendu Guha: *'More About Parsi Sheths: Their Roots, Entrepreneurship and Comprador Role, 1650-1915'*, *in* Tripathi Dwijendra (ed.): *Business Communities of India: A Historical Perspective*, p. 23-118.

58. T. R. Sharma: *Location of Industries in India*, p. 15.

59. S. M. Rutnagur: *op.cit*, p. 9.

60. J. M. Maclean: *A Guide to Bombay, (Bombay, 1877).*

61. R.P. Masani: *Dadabhoy Nowroji: The Grand Old Man of India (London, 1939)*, p. 78.

62. *Ibid.*, p. 72.

63. *Ibid.*, p. 78.

64. D. H. Buchanan: *The Development of Capitalist Enterprise in India (New York, 1934)*, p. 201.

65. R. Sullivan: *One Hundred Years of Bombay: 1836-1936(Bombay, 1936).*

66. Darryal D' Monte: *Ripping In Fabrics, The Decline of Mumbai And Its. Mill*, p. 73.

67. *G. B. C. I.* (Bombay, 1909), Vol. I, p. 168.
68. *Department of statistics, 'Index Number of Indian Prices: 1861-1918' (Calcutta 1919)*, p. 7.
69. *Imperial Gazetteer of India*, Vol. II, p. 211.
    Development Of Local Industries During (1861-65).
70. D. E. Wacha: *The Life and Life Works of J. N. Tata (Madras, 1912)*, p. 10.
71. *Indian Textile Journal (July, 1934).*
72. R. P. Masani: *Dadabhoy Nowroji, The Grand Old Man of India (London, 1939)*, p. 78.
73. *Indian Textile Journal (July , 1934).*
74. D. E. Wacha: *Op.cit.*, p. 30.
75. F. H. Harris: *The Life of J. N. Tata (London, 1925)*, p. 37.
76. *Ibid.*, pp. 35-42.
77. C. H. Rao: *Indian Biographical Dictionary*, p. 34.
78. W. W. Hunter: *Bombay 1885 to 1890: A Study in Indian Administration (London, 182)*, p. 171.
79. *Indian Cotton Textile Industry: 1851-1950, Century Volume, (Bombay, 1959)*, p. 20.
80. A. S. Pearse: *Cotton Industry of India (Manchester, 1930)*, p. 189.
81. C.H. Rao: *Op.cit.* p., 137.
82. *G.B.C.I., Op.cit.*, Vol. I, p. 401.
83. *Ibid.*, p. 168.
84. *Ibid.*, p. 304.
85. W. Digby: *Prosperous British India*, p. 185.
86. *G.B.C.I. (Bombay, 1909)*, Vol. I, p. 293
87. S. M. Rutnagur: *Op.cit.*, p. 54.
88. *Ibid.*, p. 54.
89. *Minutes of Evidence Taken before the Committee Approved to Inquire into the Indian Currency (London, 1893)*, p. 244.
90. *Ibid.*
91. *Ibid.*, p. 433.
92. V. Anstey: *The Economic Development of India (London, 1931)*, p. 114.

6

Impact of Rising Capitalist Class

(1801 – 1900 A.D.)

The account of the rise and growth of capitalist class in Bombay would not be complete if mention is not made of those Indians who received western education and became professional in their earnings. B. B. Misra calls them 'Middle Class'[1] which arose on account of the introduction of western education as per the British government's policy of liberalism in education "to promote the extension, not the monopoly of learning, to rouse the mind and elevate the character of the whole people, not to keep them in a state of slavish submission to a particular sect."[2]

It should be kept in mind that a number of natives were employed in the judicial and revenue branches of the public services and their responsibilities increased day by day. Therefore, it became indispensable for the British Government to train them in the art of administration so that they could be intellectually and morally fit to perform their duties with efficiency. Besides, the natives' employment as judicial officers and as revenue officers it became 'must' for the government to educate them because of the increasing number of civil suits on account of the replacement of customs by law. While in agricultural field, the land policy was to be executed which required these officers to define and record the rights of the different classes engaged in agriculture through survey and settlement operations. Therefore, the British Government started very seriously thinking about the Indianisation of judicial and revenue department since the days of Moira (Lord Hastings, 1813-93). In the days of Lord William Bentinck, some new posts came to be created *e.g.* Principal Sadr. Amins and Deputy Collectors, which carried emoluments to the extent of Rs. 600 to 1,000 a month.[3]

But while their responsibilities increased and their jobs became more specialized, the efforts of government to provide for their education remained limited to a few institutions of oriental learning. The Bengal Government had, for example, established a Madarasa at Calcutta, in 1781 and a Sanskrit College was established by Cornwallis at Benaras in 1792. The Indian officers of the judicial departments were recruited from among the scholars of these colleges. A similar college of Sanskrit education was established at Calcutta in 1823. Their utility was, however, restricted to law and their discipline to oriental learning. The knowledge imparted to them was not related to the growing complexity of the regulations which governed the working and constitution of the Company's courts. Nor was their training relevant to the nature of the professional skill needed in the administration of justice according to the precision of western principles and methods. As a result of this in fact the oriental learning lost most of its utility in India. In a dispatch of 1824 the Court of Directors observed that "In teaching mere Hindoo or mere Mohammadan literature you bound yourselves to teach a great deal of what was frivolous, not a little or what was purely mischievous, and a small reminder indeed in which utility was in any way concerned."[4]

Works on European literature and science was translated into original languages and made available to Indian scholars. The committee of Public Instructions which the Bengal government appointed in 1823 actually tried this, but it proved both expensive and of limited usefulness. Moreover, it had a tendency to perpetuate the traditional monopoly of literary pursuits.

Translation into local vernacular was beset with similar difficulties. On account of local and cultural variations these too involved heavy costs and restricted use. What the government wanted was to make the most extensive use of its limited resources. In 1828-29, for example, revenue amounted to £ 22 million against an annual expenditure of £ 18 million. But the Indian debt which had by that time shot upto £ 40 million, remained to be paid, as well as the payment of the Company's annuity of £ 63,00,00 in return for the surrender of its commercial privileges under the Charter Act of 1833. The Act allowed the Company to retain, as security, the whole of British territories in India for a period of twenty years.[5] Economy thus constituted a dominant consideration, and it was keeping with this that the Act divested Provincial government of their legislative and financial powers which it centralized in the supreme government of India. It was also to reduce expenses that Bentinck adopted a general plan of uniting the office of Magistrate with that of Collector. Indeed it was to meet the rising cost of administration that government had enacted regulations in 1819 and then again in 1828 to assess all such rent free lands as were held without sufficient grounds.

Economy and utility were thus two main criteria's of government policy. A scheme of translation was out of the question. Moreover, the local vernaculars were for the most part undeveloped and poor in content. They could very well be used as media of instruction for the great bulk of rural education, but even here their use presented practical difficulties. Funds were as yet too limited to admit any vernacular educational scheme being undertaken on a nationwide scale. The prejudices of caste still remained to be overcome before the benefits of education could be extended to the lower orders of society.

English education was thus considered useful and expedient as well as consistent with the political requirements of British rule in India. But although the basic policy of government was to widen its scope, practical considerations demanded that it should be limited to the upper and middle classes of urban society. It was believed that these classes, because of their previous monopoly of educational facilities, wealth and influence, could more easily be trained as teachers, and that once they had received western education, they might educate their countrymen in their own language. In the words of Trevelyan, "The rich, the learned, the men of business, will first be trained, a new class of teachers will be trained, books in the vernacular language will be multiplied, and with these accumulated means we shall in due time proceed to extend our operations from town to country, from the few to the many, until every hamlet shall be provided with its elementary school. The poor man is not the less object of the Committee's solicitude than the rich but while the means at their disposal were extremely limited, there were millions of all classes to be educated. It was absolutely necessary to make a selection, and they therefore selected the upper and middle classes as the first object of their attention. Because, by educating them first, they would soon be able to extend the same advantages to the rest of the people."[6]

By a resolution dated 7th March 1835, the Governor-General in Council therefore decided on a policy of downward filtration. It was laid down that the object of British educational policy was to promote 'European literature and science among the natives of India', and consequently all the funds appropriated for the purpose of education would best be employed on English education alone. Thomas Babington Macaulay, who shaped this policy as the President of the Committee of Public Instructions in 1835, was not unaware of its possible results. He had in fact already expressed his views in the House of Commons before he came to India as Law Member in 1836. He observed "It may be ... that, having become instructed in European knowledge they may in some future age demand European institutions. Whether such a day will ever come I know not. Whenever it comes, it will be the proudest day in English history."[7]

Before British rule, there existed both commercial and professional elements capable of growing into a capitalist class but the despotic political system of the country, its rigid caste order and monopolist economy were all inimical to its growth. The introduction of western science and technology thus involved the task of creating through English education a idle class which might act as an agency of imperialist economy and administration. It formed an integral part of British economic policy that this class should assist the operation of the imperial economy. It signified two main things, encouragement to the import of British manufactures, and incentive to the development of India's internal resources. Then only she could pay for her imports and conduce to the prosperity necessary for the purchase and consumption of foreign goods. Since the company's trade monopoly had tended to limit both these objectives, complete freedom of trade was affected by the removal of the Company's monopoly in 1833 and the transfer of the government to the Crown in 1858. However, another obstacle to the sale of British goods in India was the unchanging pattern of consumption. The dress of the people and their mode of living had remained substantially unchanged for ages, and any attempt to modify these involved a clash with local custom and caste prejudice. Charles Grant, an evangelical who retired from the Company's service in 1790, was the first to realize that an English education would be the best means of changing the old habits and the values. In his observation on the state of society, among the Asiatic subjects of Great Britain (1792), he pointed out that the communication of European knowledge through the medium of English would be "honorable and advantageous to us."[8]

Grant was in fact delighted to note the emergence of a group of English speaking Indians who had at least in some ways improved by their association with Europeans, but this effect, he commented, "is partial and not discernible in the bulk of the people, the scope for improvement was prodigious." What he meant to suggest was that with the extended use of English there would come into existence a much larger class of Indians who might co-operate with the British in the exploitation of India's resources.

Three decades later, Bishop Heber noticed discernible changes in the cultural taste of the wealthy Indians of Calcutta.

He writes that, "Their progress in the imitation of our habits (he wrote in 1823) is very apparent, though still the difference is great. None of them adopt our dress. But their houses are adorned with Verandah and Corinthian pillars, they have very handsome carriages, often built in England, they speak tolerable English, and they show a considerable liking for European society. Few of them will however eat with us."[9]

Among other things, the Parliamentary Select Committee of 1832 made inquiries about the sale of British goods in India. It came to be known that upper middle class of Calcutta had developed a taste not only for imported cotton goods but also for other articles of luxury. According to Holt Mackenzie, an able and imminent Bengal civil servant "There had been, I think, a very marked tendency among the natives to indulge in English luxuries, they have well furnished houses, many wear watches, they are fond of carriages, and are understood to drink wines."[10] When asked to account for an increasing import of European wine into India, Thomas Bracken, a partner in the house of Alexander and Company (a firm in Calcutta), told the Committee that the natives of Calcutta certainly consumed 'a great quantity of wine', for being so much with Europeans, they were divested in a much greater degree of their prejudices and habits than other. They consumed, 'wine and brandy, and beer' but the favorite wine among the natives was Champagne.[11]

These were the people who constituted elements of the new middle classes. Though not yet-class-conscious, they commanded wealth and influence. Engaged either in government offices or commerce, it was they who supported English education in Bengal. The desire to learn English was found in fewer instances in Bihar than in Bengal districts. But in both it was 'chiefly learned and wealthy men that sought it for themselves or their children, and with a view to purposes of practical utility' it was to those classes in the present condition of native society that it was 'most suitable.'[12] Macaulay had this class in view when in his Minute dated February 2, 1835, he declared, "We at present do our best to form a class who may be interpreters between us and the millions whom we govern, a class of persons Indian in blood and colour, but English in tastes, in opinions, in morals and in intellect."[13] Secondary and Higher secondary education was intended for this class, and it was with this in view that government resolved in 1835 to establish a secondary school at the headquarters of each of the districts.

Sir Charles Wood's famous Educational Dispatch dated 19th July 1854 categorically confirmed this early trend in British educational policy. As President of the Board of Control Wood stressed Western higher education through the English language. He considered this as necessary for the intellectual and moral improvement of the public servants but less significant was the emphasis on the expediency of creating a class that might do better than Europeans in the development of India's resources and increase demand for the consumption of British goods. The Wood's Dispatch clearly said that the advancement of European knowledge "will teach the natives of India the marvelous results of the employment of labour and capital, rouse them to emulate us in the development of the vast resources of their country, guide them in their efforts, and gradually, but certainly, confer upon them all the advantages which accompany the healthy increase of wealth and commerce, and at the same time secure to us a large and more certain supply of many articles necessary for our manufactures and extensively consumed by all classes of our population, as well as an almost inexhaustible demand for the produce of British labour."[14]

While the Government wished to introduce and promote English education from motives of economy, administrative expediency and liberalism, the Christian mission looked to it as an effectual means of evangelization. The Danish Lutheran missionaries were among the earliest of these. They arrived at Tanquebar in 1706, and in 1717 established two charity schools at Madras where they taught English and Christianity. Schwartz was the most distinguished of the later Danish missionaries. He established English schools at Tanjore, Ramnad, and Shivganga. In Bengal the man who provided the main incentive was Charles Grant, who on his retirement became one of the leading members of the famous Clapham sect of Evangelicals, to which men like Zachary Macaulay and Wilberforce belonged. While William Cary, J. Marshman, and W. Ward were doing pioneer missionary work in Bengal, Grant had his observations printed in 1813 and got an ecclesiastical clause inserted in the Charter Act of that year which provided for the establishment of Bishopries in India.

It appears that Marshman and Inglis were the first to advocate the use of English as a missionary agency in India. A founder of educational missions, Inglis "preached a serman in Edinburgh, in which he urged the adoption of the English language as the means for attracting the Hindus, and bringing them under the influence of the Gospel."[15]

Although English had long been in use in commercial business and its need was increasingly felt by some Indians for employment in government offices. Christian missionaries came to realize its importance in the course of their work among the half-caste Eurasian children, who grew up in ignorance and depravity, neglected by their natural European fathers and cast off by the native society to which their mother belonged. In both Calcutta and Bombay, institutional attempts at English education began for these half-caste children and later extended to others.[16]

With reference to the above mentioned background, let us examine the development and growth of education in the Bombay city and Island. The credit for the starting of early education in Bombay goes to the Christian missionaries. At the close of sixteenth century, the Gazetteer of Bombay City and Island records that the Franciscan fathers maintained three Parochial schools for catechism and rudimentary instructions in Latin and Portuguese. One was attached to the Church of Nossa Senhora da Esperanca which was built in 1596 and a second to the Church of Nossa Senhora de Gloria in Mazgaon. The third was attached to the Church of Mahim which was perhaps identical, with the so called Mahim College and which was abandoned about 1810. It was finally demolished in 1851. At the zenith of Portuguese dominion, it ranked as the chief

Portuguese college in Western India, but was subsequently transformed into a seminary for Portuguese youths.[17] More than a hundred year before, the island of Bombay was ceded to the English Crown, and the Portuguese had founded an orphanage at Montpezier in Salsette for the education of destitute native children. It continued for nearly two centuries. The other similar institutions were founded in Agasi, Karanja (Uran) and near Thane at a village which has now been covered by Vihar lake.[18]

All these institutions gave an elementary education in Portuguese and Latin. A considerable number of parochial elementary schools were also maintained at Bombay and on the adjacent islands by the Franciscans and Jesuit Orders but these were inferior in grade to the orphanages. The colleges for higher instructions were also established at Bassein, Thane and Chaul. The Institution of Bassein which was founded in 1548 had theological seminary attached to it and gave high order of education to students. Dr. John Fryer, who visited Bombay in the year 1674 had high opinion about these institutions and added that the Bassein College had an extensive library of historical, moral and expository works.[19]

A well known fact of history is that the Portuguese were expelled by the Marathas when later got victory over former in 1739. As a result of this event the Catholic orders were suppressed which included the orphanages and colleges. However, the parochial schools still survived and were carried on by native clergy with the aid of private liberal persons. An attempt was made by Sir Miquel de Lima to establish a college at Bombay towards the end of the century but his attempt failed. It was not until the return of the Jesuits to Bombay that the re-establishment of a complete system of school was taken up shortly before the foundation of Bombay University. In 1795 a school was founded by Antonio de Souza for the free education of Roman Catholic children of Mazgaon who were taught only Portuguese and Latin.[20]

After the cession of the island to the English, the first educational institution founded was a charity school, opened by Reverend Richard Cobbe, Chaplain of St. Thomas Church, in the fort in September 1718 with the object of "Educating poor (European) children in the Christian religion, according to the use of the Church of England." The success of this school was probably responsible for the Court of Directors recommending to the Bombay Government in 1752 "the setting up and establishing of charity schools wherein the children of soldiers, mariners and other might be educated, as well of the subordinates as at Bombay." A subsequent order laid down that "bastards, and the children of slaves on one side should be admitted, provided the other children would mix with them."[21]

Under the able guidance of Reverend R. Cobbe, the inhabitants of Bombay raised fund to the tune of Rs. 6,000 to which the governor Charles Boone generously donated Rs. 2,000 expecting that the East India Company would come to the further assistance. However, it was in 1767 that Mrs. Eleanor donated Rs. 6,000 which was kept in Company's treasury for nearly 57 years and thus with interest it got accumulated to the tune of Rs. 46,000. In 1807, the Court of Directors took up the school under their own management and finally in 1815 handed it over to the "Society for Promoting the Education of the Poor within the government of Bombay" which was founded in 1815 and was known as the Bombay Education Society.[22] This society was the first of its kind in India which received nearly a lakh of rupees as donations during the first five years of its existence and was warmly supported by the National Society in England. It did not confine its efforts only to the education of European children but extended its operation even beyond the island. This society encouraged the native boys to attend schools and thus by 1820, the Society had opened four schools for natives in the island attended by about 250 pupils. In the month of August same year, this Society formed a separate branch known as the Elphinston Native Education Institution whose object was to prepare school books in the vernacular languages and to aid in establishing vernacular schools.[23] However, two years later the Society confined itself solely to the education of European and Eurasian children as it could not bear the responsibility that had increased. It severed itself from the Elphinston Native Education Institution which since then bore the responsibility of the education of the native population under the title of "The Bombay Native School Book and School Society." It was this Society only which came to be known as The Bombay Native Education Society in 1827. In 1840, it was merged with a Board of Education which carried out the responsibility of educational administration in Bombay in share with the missionary bodies from Europe and America.

Among the earliest missionaries who did pioneer work in the field of education was the American Marathi Mission. It arrived in Bombay in 1813 and in May 1815 opened a Hindu boy's school which was the first school conducted on Western lines. After this they opened a girl's school in 1824 and within two years they registered an increase of 9 girl's schools attended by 340 pupils and in 1829 by 400 pupils of whom 122 were able to read and write and do plain needle work. One of these institutions was a boarding school which was successfully maintained at Byculla for several years. The Governor of Bombay and many high officials subscribed liberally to the American Marathi Mission School funds.[24] Gradually, the American Marathi Mission left its work in Bombay for opening new educational centers in Ahmednagar. In the meanwhile, the Church Missionary Society appeared in the field and in 1820 opened their first school for native girls and in 1835 founded Anglo-Vernacular School in memory of Robert Cotton Money who was Secretary to the government in education department and was also Secretary to the Native Education Society. The school of this Society went on making advancement till 1840 when it got sudden setback in the number of pupils on account of the baptisation of two of its pupils. But it was just a temporary phase because by 1852, the numbers of the pupils were again on rise in Robert Money School. Among the other missionaries, mention must be made of Dr. John Wilson of Scottish Missionary Society who established six schools for native girls assisted by his wife Mrs. Wilson between 1829 to 1830. In 1830, Dr. John Wilson opened a school for boys which was financed by local contributions and in which both English and vernacular languages were taught.

Meanwhile the Bombay Native Education Society went on making progress due to the encouragement given by Honourable Mountstuart Elphinston who was an advocate of both higher and vernacular education. This was the reason why when he left his office in 1827 the native chiefs of Deccan and Konkan as well as the public raised more than 2½ lakhs to found a Presidency college to commemorate his memory. Later this money got accumulated to nearly 4½ lakhs of rupees. The Bombay Government undertook to superintend the general maintenance of the college. However, in the year 1840 the Government decided to amalgamate the school and college classes into one institution named the Elphinston Institution and placed it under a Board of Education comprised of a President and three European members appointed by the Native Education Society that since then disappeared from the educational field. The first members of the board of Education were Sir J. W. Awdry, Messrs. Bruce, Morris (Secretary to government), Dr. J. Maclean (afterwards Physician General in Bombay) and Messrs. Jagannath Shankar Seth, Mohammad Ibrahim Makba and Jamshetji Jeejibhoy.[25] This Board of Education was entirely responsible for the whole educational administration of the Bombay Presidency until the State recognized the need of a properly organized Department of Public Instruction. Till the organization of the Department of Public Instructions the board of Education looked after the schools in Bombay island which comprised the Elphinston Institution and seven vernacular schools in 1840.[26] The first step of the State government was to divide the Presidency into three educational divisions each under a European Inspector with one native assistant and after this the School Committees were established. The government also founded a Normal class which moved very slowly on the death of its first Director, Bal Gangadhar Shastri and was finally abolished around 1848. A Surveying and Civil Engineering Class was added to the upper division of the Elphinston Institution in 1844 under a European

Professor chosen in England by the Court of Director. In 1846 a Professor of Botany and Chemistry was also appointed together with a Special Committee for the preparation of English and Vernacular text books. The Board also received control of the Grant Medical College founded in 1845. The most notable President of the Board was Sir Erskine Perry, Chief Justice (1843-52) whose encouragement of higher education involved a deviation from the previous tendency of the educational movement in Bombay, and whose policy so stimulated private enterprise that by the end of his tenure of office nine private English schools were being maintained by their promoters in the capital of the Presidency. Besides these, "there were 17 indigenous schools in the Fort, of which 12 belonged to Hindus and 5 to Parsis, and 75 vernacular schools outside the limits of the Fort, including both government, missionary and indigenous institutions, the total number of boys receiving English or Vernacular Education was reported to be 5809."

Writing in 1848, Lady Falkland remarks: "There are several other admirable schools and institutions for purposes of education some supported by government, or by the various missionary bodies, others supported by natives amongst which later are some very large Parsi Schools."

The Gazetteer of Bombay City and Island also records that "The indigenous schools were chiefly owned by a so-called Mehtaji, who held their classes on the Varandah of a house, free of rent. Chairs and tables were unknown, and very few pupils possessed slates or pencils, their place being supplied by a portable wooden board, on which the pupil wrote with a reed pen dipped in chalky fluid and which was repainted every Diwali by the Mehtaji for a small consideration. The Mehtaji exercised unlimited power within his own domain. Not only did he oblige his elder pupils to sweep the school premises every morning, but in case of misbehaviour, he subjected the boys to sever and most ingenious mode of punishment, such as standing in a bent position for an hour with their fingers touching their toes. The arrival of a few pupils was an occasion of a regular initiation ceremony in which the Mehtaji, after being garlanded at the house of the boy's parents, headed a procession back to school, amid the chanting of hyms to Ganesh, the god of knowledge. This was followed by the distribution of inkstands and sweetmeats to the pupils, who observed the remainder of the day as a holiday. Bombay also contained a few private academies of an exclusive character, attended by the sons of the rich, in which the fees were high, discipline was lax, and the pupils studied or not according to their own fancy."[27]

After Sir Erskine Perry's retirement from the Board in 1852 the Government's subsidy to primary education got increased to 2½ lakhs. As a result of this board undertook to open a school in any village of the Presidency provided the inhabitants of the villages were ready to bear half of the salary of the teacher and to provide a school room and class books. The Board laid the foundation of a system of education which in many respects anticipated the principles of the famous Wood's dispatch of 1854. Thus was prepared the way for establishing of an university, by the establishment of institutions for the teaching of literature, law, medicine and civil engineering. It also introduced a system of primary schools, administered by the State, but mainly supported by the people themselves, which formed the germs of the modern local fund system.

At the time of the transfer of the functions of the Board to the Director of Public Instruction in 1855, the number of government institutions in Bombay Island was ten, namely the Elphinstone Institution and two branch schools six vernacular schools and the Grant Medical College, which was founded in 1845. The chief private institutions at this date were the Bombay Education Society's Boy's and Girl's schools, the Indo-British Institution, the Bombay Scotish Orphanage, the St. Mary's Institution, the Convent School at Parel, Sir J. J. Parsi Benevolent Institution, several school of American mission, the Robert Money School and 12 vernacular schools belonging to the Church Missionary Society, and the Scotish Missionary

Society's schools. Sectarian education was represented by the Prabhu seminary and a Bhatia school also attended by Khojas, Memons and Lohanas. While female education was stimulated by the Students Literary and Scientific Society which supported nine vernacular free schools for girls. The Students Literary and Scientific Society was formed by Professor Patton of the Elphinston College in 1848 and this society alone maintained 16 schools with 1132 pupils, including several female schools with 120 pupils. Mohammadan education was represented by only one Hindustani school opened by the government in Kazi Street in 1834 because the bulk of the Mohammadan population had no desire for education on Western lines and was quite content with the ability to read or recite the Koran. The only exception to this was Mohammed Ibrahim Makba, a Konkani Mohammadan, who was elected as a member of the Managing Committee of the Native Education Society in 1822 and became a member of Elphinston College Council in 1834. He also became a member of Board of Education in 1840 and was instrumental in popularizing the first Mohammadan School opened in 1834.

The orders on the 'Dispatch' was sent by the government of India to the government of Bombay in February 1855 and three months later the Department of Public Instruction was formed. Mr. C. J. Erskine became its first Director and Dr. Harkness, Principal of the Elphinston College, was appointed as first Education Inspector of the Presidency. Rao Bahadur V.N. Mandlik was made responsible for the inspection of the vernacular schools in the island as deputy Education Inspector of the Thane and Kolaba districts. Mr. Erskine's first act was to prepare an inspection code prescribing the conditions under which grants were to be paid to private schools and provided for a system of stipendiary scholarships. He further provided for an entrance test for higher primary and for secondary and collegiate institutions, and was about to deal with the question of augmenting the number of trained teachers for vernacular schools, when due to ill health he resigned from his office. He was succeed by Mr. Howard who devoted himself mainly to the consolidation of the departmental system, prepared the colleges and higher schools for the university and secured the voluntary aid of the people in the improvement rather than the extension of primary schools. However, due to the outbreak of the Mutiny of 1857 all works except war claims came to be stopped which again could not be resumed before 1865. During the regime of Mr. Howard, the educational institutions like the government Central Museum (Victoria and Albert Museum), the David Sassoon Industrial and Reformatory Institution, Sir Jamshedji Jijibhoy Institute of Art and the University of Bombay, which held the first matriculation examination in October, 1859, came to be established.

With the establishment of the University of Bombay in 1857, the city actually marched towards the growth of the modern Western education. The foundation of such western education, though, was laid by the benevolent Mountstuart Elphinston (Governor of Bombay; 1819-27), the real headway towards the progress came to be commenced in the fifties of the nineteenth century when the intelligentia of Bombay initiated the process of national awakening. The intelligentia of the period is defined by Christine Dobin "As all those in Bombay, who received English education in the collegiate classes of the Elphinston Institution before the founding of the University, and those who gained University degrees after that date. The term also comprises those who attended professional institutions, such as the Grant Medical College and the Government Law Classes."[28] The University of Bombay founded in 1857 on the model of London university not only formalized the educational structure in Bombay but also gave birth to intelligentia whom B. B. Misra calls as 'Middle class.'[29]

Jagannath Shankar Sheth and Dr. Bhaudaji Lad played a very active and important role in the foundation of University of Bombay and became its Fellows by an act of incorporation of the University. The other Indians who became Fellows were Sir Jamshedji Jijibhoy, Bomanji Hormusji and Mohammad Yusuf Moorgay. Jagannath Shankar Sheth remained as a member of the Senate since its foundation till his death in 1865. Dadabhoy Nawroji, a product of the renaissance was also one of the founders of university. Sir Alexander Grant, John Wilson, Justice James Gibbs, Sir Raymond West, Dr. Mackichan and many other enlightened Europeans devoted themselves to the mission of educational expansion in Bombay which had profound effect on all-round growth of the city.

The first four graduates of the University were Mahadeo Govind Ranade, Ramakrishna Gopal Bhandarkar, Bal Mangesh Wagle and Vaman Abaji Modak who were awarded B. A. Degrees in 1862 and became distinguished persons of the times. They were shortly joined by Pherozshah Merwanji Mehta (1864), Kashinath Trimbak Telang (1867) and Rahimtulla Mohammad Sayani (1868), Balshastri Gangadhar Jambhekar, Atmaram Pandurang, Parmanand Vishwanath, Narayan Mandlik who all formed the class of intelligentia. The Parsis were just beginning to emerge from their mercantile activities. Pherozshah Mehta, Dinshaw Edulji Wacha, Nawroji Furdunji and Shorabji Sapurji Bengali emerged on the scene and enriched the elite in Bombay under the inspiring guidance of Dadabhai Nawroji. It was this glaxy of luminaries who became responsible for rising social and political awakening in Bombay by becoming precursors of the intelligentia.

In the forties of the nineteenth century, Sir Erskine was associated with the spread of education in the Bombay Presidency as President of the Board of Education. He did pioneering work in the field of education in Bombay where he found the growth of a true intellectual awakening followed by a rising public spirit and closer communication between the rulers and the ruled.[30]

The controversy that arose in connection with the medium of instruction came to be resolved by Wood's Dispatch in 1854 which decided the higher education to be imparted through English language but laid more emphasis on vernacular institutions to the masses. The aim of the Government to impart higher education in English was to rise up a class of Indian 'Gentlemen' and to train the best class of natives suitable for government service. The government intended to associate the rich businessmen (Shetias) with the educational plan[31] but they took no interest in new education, except a few. Therefore the English education remained mainly confined to Brahmins and other literary castes and middle class Parsis.[32] But the fact remains that some rich businessman did patronize the education either privately helping poor students or founding Anglo-Vernacular schools as did Jagannath Shankar Sheth, Gokuldas Tejpal and Varjivandas Madhavdas or endowing the Bombay University with buildings and scholarships like Sir Cowasji Jahangir Ready money (who received Knighthood in 1875), Premchand Roychand and Sir Mangaldas Nathubhai.

The Elphinston College produced a good number of persons who made an important mark in the life of the Bombay city and of the country.[33] Among the teachers in the college were Balshastri Jambhekar (1812-46), and Nawroji Furdunji (1817-85). The later distinguished himself as one of the architects of the political organizations in Bombay. Jambhekar was an acting Professor of Mathematics in 1842. In 1845, Dadabhai Nawroji (1825-1917) was appointed as acting Professor of Mathematics and Natural Philosophy. Of a later generation M. G. Ranade (1842-1901) was appointed Professor of English, R. G. Bhandarkar (1837-1925) as Professor of Oriental Languages in the Elphinston College and B. M. Wagle at Poona College which was founded in 1821 and was renamed as Deccan College in 1867.

Later on some other notable and distinguished students of Elphinston College played an excellent role in the social and political history of Bombay. One of them was Dr. Bhau Daji Lad (1822-74) who became one of the Bombay's first medical graduate from the Grant Medical College. He was one of the most active member of the Bombay Association of which he was the Secretary for many years and played an outstanding role in the political life of the Bombay city. R. N. Khot (1821-91), who became extremely rich through trade, was a great conservative in the politics of Bombay. Atmaram Pandurang Tarkhadkar (1823-98) distinguished himself in medical studies and was the founder of Prarthana Samaj.[34] S. S. Bengali (1831-93) was a Parsi who was a noted journalist, political activist and social reformer of Bombay. Kharshedji Rustomji Cama was another intellectual who did researches in the Zoroastrian religion and was held in high esteem among the intelligentia.

Another most noteworthy Elphinstonians included V. N. Mandlik (1833-89), who later distinguished himself by playing many roles in Bombay's political history, particularly as a pioneering Marathi journalist and political activist. Javerilal Umashankar achieved highest academic honours in the college and became a leading Gujarati political figure. Narmada Shankar Lalshankar (1833-86), a Gujarati poet, and Karsandas Mulji (1832-71) a Bania reformer, were among those who adorned the public life of the city of Bombay.

The next generation of distinguished Elphinstonians included Dinshaw Edulji Wacha (1844-1936), the politician and writer who dominated the Indian National Congress politics not only in Bombay but also in India for many decades. Badruddin Tyabji (1844-1906), one of the first Muslim students, later became a leader of the Muslim community and the Indian National Congress, and a judge on the Bombay High Court. Pherozshah Merwanji Mehta (1845-1915), one of the greatest of the Bombay luminaries, a 'Lion of Bombay' and a Congress leader of unrivalled status of the day, gained his B. A. degree in 1864 and was allowed to appear for his M. A. in the same year.[35] He was instrumental in several political, municipal and social reforms, besides University reforms throughout his life. Kashinath Trimbak Telang (1850-93) who was awarded B. A. in 1868 and M. A. the following year distinguished himself at the High Court bench and the activities of the Bombay Presidency Association, as well as other political organizations. His work in the Legislative Council, civil government and Congress-politics, was outstanding. R. M. Sayani (1847-1902), Telang's contemporary was an important politician of 1880's, a congress President and Muslim leader.

The account of intelligentia would not be complete if mention is not made of the legal profession which was held in very high esteem by the Britishers, the ruling class. As the Elphinston College promoted the cause of general education in the city, the same way the Government Law College promoted the cause of legal professional course. It was the first of its kind in India, which was established in 1855 on public demand under the leadership of Jagannath Shankar Sheth. This college was affiliated to the University of Bombay in 1860 and produced a galaxy of eminent men who made history in the legal profession and national life as well. A few of them were H. J. Kania, the first Chief Justice of India, Nanabhai Haridas, the first permanent Judge of the High Court, M. G. Ranade, K. T. Telang, B. G. Tilak, Badruddin Tyabji, N. G. Chandavarkar etc. By the latter half of the nineteenth century legal profession was the only profession respected by English ruling class. Indians' admission to this profession was barred by political considerations. The rich in bombay went to England also for advanced learning in law, and ultimately gained leadership in the Bombay Intelligentia. Badruddin Tyabji, Pherozshah Mehta, G. V. Karkare, Kharshedji Manakji and Hormasji A. Wadia were among the first generation of Barristers, who formed the nucleus of an India wide fraternity. While studying in England, the Bombayites, along with Bengalis like W. C. Bannerji and Manmohan Ghose, formed a circle around Dadabhai Nawroji. Such early friendships were to prove invaluable in the political field in the following decades.[36]

In the field of medicine also, commendable work came to be done after the establishment of Grant Medical College in 1845 which was named after Robert Grant, the Governor of Bombay who originated the idea of founding a medical college in as early as 1835. The Grant Medical College awarded its first diplomas in 1845 and first degrees in 1862. From the beginning it attracted a large number of Parsis, while Hindus were repugnant to the modern system of medical education. Bhau Daji Lad and Atmaram Pandurang were among the first 15 medical graduates from this college.[37] After the Grant Medical College, the J. J. Hospital, G. T. Hospital, Cama Hospital and St. George's Hospital came to be founded. Thus the medical institutions also started adding to the class of intelligentia in the latter half of the century.

However, a point to be noted in this connection is that the Government alone was not in the field of education. The missionaries were also quite active in this field right from the beginning. The rich men *i.e.* Shetias had a different approach towards the education. While they desired to train their boys in English, they had strong dislike for their children to study in government and Mission schools. This was so because they did not like their children to get mixed up with poor children in government and Mission schools. Therefore, in order to give them some knowledge of English, they sent them to the schools run by British ex-army officers. Jagannath Shankar Sheth, D. M. Petit, Beramji Jijibhai and Mangaldas Nathubhai were educated in such school.[38] Gradually, these Shetias realized the importance of Western education and became instrumental in promoting the cause of University education from the sixtees of the nineteenth century.

As a result of support of the rich businessmen and also due to state government upliftment of higher education, the number of pass outs from the University increased in the city and island of Bombay. The decade wide growth in the number of pass outs has been given in the following Table.[39]

Number of Pass Outs

Examination	*1864-73*	*1889-94*
B.A.	168	1,464
Honors and M.A.	034	0032
Law	033	0244
Medicine	094	0172
Civil Engineering	083	0024
Total	412	1,936

The above Table shows increase in the number of pass outs in all examinations during 1864-73. However, in the five years between1889-94 the increase was much higher, particularly in the field of law and medicine. It is noteworthy that during the year 1864-73 the number of pass outs in law was just 33 and in medicine 94 while during five years between 1889-94 the number of pass out in law and medicine was 244 and 172 respectively. However, the number of pass outs in Civil Engineering examination shows considerable decline from the block year between 1864-73 to block year 1889-94. This decline perhaps was due to the neglect of technical education before the general education. Whatever the reason be for this, one fact that comes out of this analysis is that the number of the class of elite did rise considerably in the latter half of the nineteenth century and they were bound to play their destined role in the history of not only Bombay but also in the country.

The figures that are worth examining are also of those who adopted legal profession. Upto 1870, the number of Advocates in Bombay was just nine and Vakils eighteen while their number went on increasing with every decade. The following table shows this increased number.[40]

Year	*Advocates*	*Vakils*
Upto 1870	009	018
1871-1880	025	076
1881-1890	042	082
1891-1900	100	198
Total ...	176	374

The above Table indicates that increased number of 176 Advocates in Bombay, 108 were Indians, of whom 54 were Parsis. The remaining 68 were Europeans, Anglo-Indians and others. Prominent among the Indians in the list were Pherozshah Mehta in 1868, Mohandas Karamchand Gandhi in 1892, Mohammad Ali Jina in 1896 and Vallabhbhai Patel in 1899. They were all barristers and advocates of Bombay High Court. The Vakils of this Court were for the most part Hindus, with a fair sprinkling of Parsis. Below them came Attorneys and Solicitors who were largely Anglo-Indians and the Parsis. Then came the Pleaders who were mainly Hindus and practiced in districts and subordinate courts."[41]

In the light of the above discussion, it has becomes amply clear that the emerging professional capitalist class in the city and island of Bombay was bound to effect the changes as they were all the product of modern education. The most remarkable change that they brought about was on the hereditary status of caste. Although the nineteenth century's religious reformers also tried to shake the hold of casteism but their influence could not be so much as this newly emerged educated class could shake the traditional social order. This could be possible because of the Western education as well as the capitalist economy with a free judiciary and parliamentary education.

The western education had its effects in three ways. *Firstly,* it broke the intellectual monopoly of the Brahmins by opening the doors to all classes. *Secondly,* it created an educated class of Indians who became supporters of liberal reforms and *thirdly,* it set into motion the degree of occupational mobility due to which the social mobility got increased. Since, in the traditional casè order learning remained with the Brahmins and crafts with the artisans, the Western education brought about a synthesis of the two by giving equal opportunity to both incase of changing their professions. Thus, the Western education not only gave the ideological principle of liberalism but also created a new class to follow that principle. Although the effort in this direction was made earlier through the religious movements but due to the monopolization of education no new class could emerge to support that ideal or put the same into practice.

The influence of the modern legal and judicial system was much more deeper. The Hinduism was modified not in schools and colleges but in law courts. It was the law courts that leveled the distinctions based on caste. The legal luminaries were not only the protectors of persons and their property but they also acted as the watchdogs of their civil liberty. The professional duty of the new class of legal practitioners demanded conformity with the rule of law. The professional discipline which regulated their conduct made them liable to prosecution in the event of their failure to serve their clients regardless of caste or religious pursuation of their own. Thus, the institution of British courts in India brought into being a class of persons who were not to refuse legal assistance to anyone whosoever required it.

It was a consequence of the British economic order of Laissez-fair and of the British educational and legal system that the state was duty bound not only to uphold a free economic system but also to protect and promote the interest of individuals in the pursuit of that system. With certain modifications, the British transplanted India, the relationship which had come to subsist between business and government at home. The various Chambers of Commerce, Trade Associations, and bodies of mill owners obliged the Government to remove trade barriers, to improve communications, and to affect land, police and judicial reforms so as to ensure the security of property. The introduction of a free press and representative government was also to some extent motivated by the consideration of reducing the authority of the executive in the interest of free trade.To these must be added the professionalization of modern business and the influence exercised by financial trusts, the Directors of Industry and their personnel, all resulting from the growth of capitalism.

But these changes were only in the cities and large towns. Its effects were never felt on rural areas that constituted 80 percent of the rural population. The operation of the imperialist economy limited the growth of Indian capitalism because it was in the interest of British to maintain the Indian bureaucracy's myth of superiority which was always dominated by the Europeans at higher level. Since the traditional caste authoritarianism well fitted the imperial policy and the Indian bureaucrats belonged usually to higher caste, they toed the line of the British only.

Although the professional men were opposed to the extension of tenants and labour reforms, they did advocate the development of indigenous capitalism. As a result of the occupational mobilization many members of the higher caste, including Brahmins, developed interests in modern trade and industry. Some of them became the leaders of education and business. This occupational mobility was of great social significance. It led to effect a radical change in the traditional relationship of the literary and business classes. The intellectuals and the plutocrats, who had in the past pulled in opposite directions, were under the British being drawn close together. Their coming together was due to the political reason for the British rule thwarted the aspirations of the educated Indians by excluding them from higher posts in the civil service. It prejudiced the interests of the Indian capitalists by denying them their rights to protection. Therefore, the growth of an alliance between the intelligentia and the business men was of considerable importance.

The Indian National Congress Party naturally became the rallying ground for the educated as well as for the business classes. Of the total number of 1,584 delegates, who attended Poona Session of the Indian National Congress in 1895, as many as 437 were member of the commercial classes. The number of business representatives who attended the Calcutta Session in 1896 was 88 only, but at the 1906 Calcutta Session it was 230.[42]

Men like Dadabhai Nawroji and G. K. Ghokhle were not business men, but they agitated for the development of indigenous capitalist enterprise. They believed that the operation of the imperialist economy obstructed the pace of India's industrial progress, for although it encouraged agricultural and commercial development the dominance of the import industry had the effect of destroying the country's artisan production without promoting a corresponding increase in the output of mill made goods. The paucity of indigenous capital, technical skill, and enterprise partly accounted for the state of industrial backwardness. It constituted a serious strain on India's financial resources, and much of the trade balance which might have otherwise contributed to industrial advancement went towards the payment of the 'Home charges'.

M. N. Roy writes that "Economic necessities forced the intellectual bourgeoisie to begin its political struggle, which was initiated in form of the Indian National Congress, whose first Session, was held in 1885 in Bombay, under the Presidency of W. C. Banerji, a rich lawyer who had his savings invested in commercial and industrial enterprises. The object of this political movement was manifest. It was to replace or at least to curtail the power of the British government, which was standing in the way of the economic development of the bourgeoisie. This movement was headed by rich lawyers, merchants, mill owners, physicians etc., or in other words, that progressive element of the society which possessed capital to be invested."[43] He further comments that "The economic power of the Indian bourgeoisie, composed of the intellectuals, mercantile capitalists, liberal land holders, and the industrial capitalists, had acquired sufficient strength to enable it to declare an open struggle against the foreign capitalistic monopoly."[44]

Perhaps this was the reason why a certain section of British administrators realized that the earlier policy of creating a class of educated Indians had been a mistake on their part. Because once this class began to grow in stature, a demand for an equal share in the administration of the country began. Refusal to recognize their claims caused bitterness and disaffection. Perhaps to rectify that error attempts were made to retard the progress of higher education partly by an emphasis on primary education but more by limiting the responsibility of the State in the advancement of the education as a whole. This is very clear from the Presidential Address delivered by Lord Curzon at an educational conference held at Shimla on 6th September 1901. "There exists (he said), a powerful school of opinion which does not-hide its conviction that the experiment (of English education) was a mistake, and that its result has been disaster. When Erasmus was reproached with having laid the egg from which came forth the Reformation. 'Yes', he replied, 'but I laid a hen's egg, and Luther has hatched a fighting cock'. This, I believe, is pretty much the view of a good many of the critics of English education in India. They think that it has given birth to a tone of mind and to a type of character that is ill regulated, averse from discipline, discontented, and in some causes actually disloyal."[45]

Thus the British rule in Bombay, like elsewhere in India, became responsible for the educational development particularly the Western education that gave rise to the intelligentia class and it was this class that firstly became conscious of the ill effects of the British rule. They started making their efforts to generate the awareness among the masses socially and politically against the foreign rule and thus became responsible for creating a united front against the foreign masters. When the Britishers realized their mistake they started clasping their hold over the educational institutions particularly from the beginning of the twentieth century but finally they were destined to quit the country in 1947. The labour of the intellectuals was amply rewarded.

REFERENCES

1. B. B. Misra: *The Indian Middle Classes (1983)*, p. 149.
2. C.E. Trevelyan: *On the Education of the People of India (London, 1838)*, pp. 135-6.
3. B. B. Misra: *Op.cit.*, p. 149.
4. H. Sharp: *Selection From Educational Records, Pt-I (1920)*, p. 92.
5. B.B. Misra: *Op.cit.*, p. 150.
6. C.E. Trevelyan: *Op.cit.*, p. 48.
7. Quoted by B.B. Misra in *The Indian Middle Classes*, p. 152.
8. *Report of Select Committee of Hourse of Commons 1831-32, Gen, App.*
9. Quoted by B. B. Misra in *The Indian Middle Classes*, p. 153.
10. *Report of Select Committee of House of Commons, 1831-32, Minutes, of Ev. II (735-II)*, p. 11.
11. *Ibid.*
12. Adam, William: *Adam's Reports on Vernacular Education in Bengal and Bihar, Submitted to Government in 1835, 1836 and 1838*, p. 219.
13. Quoted by B.B. Misra in *The Indian Middle Classes*, p.154.
14. *Ibid.*, p. 154.

15. Rev. J. Johnstone: *Abstract and Analysis of the Report of the Indian Education Commission (London, 1884)*, p. 11.
16. *Ibid.*, p. 12.
17. *Bombay Times, October 22nd, 1851.*
18. *G.B.C.I. (1910)*, Vol. III, p. 99.
19. *Ibid.*, p. 100.
20. *Ibid.*
21. *Bombay Quarterly Review-II*, p. 101.
22. *Ibid.*
23. Christine Dobin: *Urban Leadership in Western India – Politics and Communities in Bombay City, 1840-1885 (Oxford University Press, Oxford, 1971)*, p. 57.
24. *G.B.C.I. Op.cit.*, Vol. III, p. 102.
25. *Ibid.*, Vol. III, p. 105.
26. *Ibid.*
27. *The late Mr. K.N. Kabraji's Reminiscences, represented in Times of India, 1901, G.B.C.I.*, Vol. III, p. 106.
28. Christine Dobin: *Op.cit.*, p. 28.
29. B.B. Misra: *Op.cit.*, p. 149.
30. *Official Report of the Board of Education, Bombay 1849, app, III*, pp. 69-91.
31. *Ibid.*
32. *The Gazetteer of Maharashtra State – Greater Bombay District, Vol. I, 1986.*
33. Christine Dobin: *Op.cit.*, p. 36.
34. *First Report of the Elphinstone Native Education Institution, 1840.*
35. Homi Modi: *Sir Pherozshah Mehta: A Political Biography (Asia Publishing House, London, reprinted in 1963)*, p. 192.
36. Christine Dobin: *Op.cit.*, p. 47.
37. *Ibid.*, p. 48.
38. *Times of India, 4th Feb, 1884.*
39. B.B. Misra: *Op.cit.*, pp. 300-301.
40. *Thacker's Industrial Directory -1901*, p. 1172-3, *given in* B.B. Misra: *The Indian Middle Classes*, p. 328.

41. *Ibid.*, pp. 328-329.
42. *Ibid.*, p. 357.
43. M. N. Roy: *India in transition (1917)*, p. 27.
44. *Ibid.*, p. 28.
45. *Curzon of Kedleston, Marquis of Lord Curzon in India, being a Selection from his Speeches as Viceroy and G.G. of India, 1888-1905, ed. By Sir T. Raleigh London (1906)*, pp. 315-16.

7

Nature and Strength of Capitalist Class

In the Western part of India, Bombay became the commercial and political stronghold of the East Indian Company and the British came to have very strong commercial relationship with merchants of this island. It was acquired by the British Crown in 1661 and was handed over to the East India Company in 1667 for a symbolic sum of £ 10. Since then Bombay became the main factory of British and the importance of Surat declined. In September 1668, the Council at Surat recorded the Company's intention. "It is being the Honourable Company's desire that we contrive the best way for making Bombay a port for the exportation and importation of goods and persons to and from Persia, Mocha and other parts."[1] The document also expresses the desire to set up a shipyard in Bombay, where timber, iron works, carpenters and many other materials "are very cheap, the buildings far more substantial than in England." Besides, the money expended on pay for the shipbuildings "will remain in the island and the people and the people be the better able to pay those duties and rent annually received from them."[2]

In the 18th century, the importance of Gujarat ports started declining and the foreign trade and feudal disorders undermined the economy of the towns like Ahmadabad. The trade routes were paralyzed by countless transit levies and military raids.[3] According to Forbes once everything had been in favour of Ahmadabad's trade, which was assemblage of merchants, handicraft men and travelers from various countries, in contrast to the scene of devastations and neglect which it presented in 1789. In 1817, a British official reported that in Ahmadabad he found a sad scene of destruction.[4] Under the changed circumstances, the local merchants began to move to Bombay which was controlled by the Marathas. Since without the help of local intermediary, it was not possible for the East India Company to trade the brokerage of the local merchants became absolutely inevitable. That was why the Company was forced to allow the settlers to settle on the island of Bombay relatively on advantageous terms. Thus, when in the late 17th century, the Company invited the Banias of Surat to move to Bombay, the later bargained and secured a number of privileges for themselves.[5] Together with the Hindu Banias the Parsis also moved to Bombay.

In a letter dated July 1677, the Bombay Factors requested their colleagues in Surat to find a coiner by the name of Ratanji, who "is an able workman, which will be of great benefit in making all the money of a true and equal weight," and to send him as fast as possible to Bombay.[6] In the early 1740s, Cawasji Cama moved to Bombay among others and established the shipbuilding industry there, and so did Rustomji Dorabji, whom the British subsequently appointed the Patel of Bombay.[7] S. M. Edwardes appears to be wrong when he maintains that Lawji Nassurvanji Wadia "had been connected with the Island since the year 1692, when he assisted with a body of Kolis to repeal the invasion of Siddi. For this good work, he was appointed by the government Patel of Bombay."[8] Wadia could not have performed such a feat in 1692 both because of his age (for he died in 1772) and because of his status in opinion of V. I. Pavlov.

The Gujarati Parsis were given a special tract of land on Malabar Hill in 1773 in the centre of Bombay.[9] By 1780, there were already 3,000 Parsis in Bombay, and within ten years many more Parsis came to live in Bombay to escape the famine in Gujarat. Between the periods 1770 to 1780, according to Forbes, the Parsis owned sizeable area of land and fine houses in Bombay. They either built the houses themselves or bought them from the British who were leaving for home. The enterprising nature of new settlers enabled them to have their own firms so much so that in the early 19th century out of 53 firms registered at Bombay. 37 of them were owned by the Indians.[10] However, despite the fact that the Indian owners of the firms were more than the Europeans; their commercial operations were controlled by the British merchant capital.

In the early 18th century, the East India Company carried on its trade in Bombay through its official brokers. During the period of war between the Marathas and the Mughals, the British co-operated with the Bombay merchants by allowing them to sell the goods in the inland areas and prohibited the Company's employees from selling the goods. Thus, there existed a good deal of co-operation between the East India Company and the Bombay merchants.

The brokerage system came to be abolished by 1737 as the ties between the local merchants got strengthened hence many Bombay traders became partners of British firms subsequently. According to W. Hamilton, every European trading establishment had a Parsi partner, who usually provided most of the capital and their services were much valued by the British firms.[11] This is very clear from the incident of Hormusji who lost huge sum of 2,00,000 pounds as a result of speculation and he was helped by the firm of Charles Forbes with whom the former had a very close business ties. Apart from supplying the provisions to the Bombay garrison and Company's fleet, the Bombay merchants also traded with the Middle East under the escort of British men-of-war. When the Company's Council abolished the system of escorting Indian merchants, the three Hindu merchants, opposed this move by filling a petition to the Company's authorities on the ground that the stoppage of the system of escorting would prove ruinous for the commercial interests and thus relation with the British would also be strained. Therefore, the Company had to reserve its decision for it could never afford to lose the co-operation of Indian merchants.

Gujarat's trade with China was of special importance to the East India Company because the Indian opium and cotton was exported from Gujarat to China. In the second half of the 18th century, Gujarat also exported cotton to Bengal and all these trades were controlled by the Bombay merchants, the British and the Guajaratis who concluded contracts with native merchants buying up the cotton in the villages.[12] J. Douglas informs us that in 1801 seven Bombay merchants bought a consignment of cotton worth 3,50,000 rupees for dispatch to China out of which three of them were Englishmen and four Parsi merchants.[13]

At the close of the 18th century and beginning of the 19th century, commerce with China was the principal item in the turnover of Bombay. For example, in 1805, the export to China reached 6,473,600 rupees, and to Great Britain only 5,08,700 rupees.[14] However, this does not mean that the trade remained confined to China only. In fact, the export of cotton, and later of opium, to China was the principal source from which the Company acquired its silver coin with which it purchased the Indian export goods in Bengal and elsewhere.

The rise of Bombay's shipping occurred due to the trade with China and other Asian countries. The Parsis began to take interest in shipping in 1735. By 1792, the Parsis owned more than 20 big ships (mainly built in Bombay). The biggest Ship Masters were members of the Wadia family, who possessed six vessels, and members of the Ready money family, who had three vessels. Members of the Ready money (the ancestors of K. N. Davar, the first mill owner of Bombay) were also among the first ship masters of Bombay.[15] During the second half of the 18th century and the beginning of the 19th century, the principal source of the wealth of Bombay merchants was shipping revenue.

Thus, it becomes evidently clear that the Gujarat merchants made good fortune and acquired considerable wealth by acting in collaboration with their British partners. The Englishmen John Burnell, who visited India in 1711, wrote "The Banias or merchants are not only rich and wealthy, but like the rest of the world are covetous after more, placing the height of their happiness in riches, which they will scrape together by mean and petty offices, some of them amassing prodigious sums of money, being accounted worth 90 or 100 lakhs, or so many a times Rs. 1,00,000."[16] Evidence regarding the enormous riches accumulated by the Gujarati merchants co-operating with English is confirmed by documentary material. In 1721, after the death of a well known Company broker Rustomji Manekji his heir demanded the return of a loan amounting to Rs. 6,90,000 from the East India Company. After the Bombay Council of the Company refused to pay back the money, one of Manek's sons got Board of Directors to agree to reconsider the matter. Consequently, Manekji's heirs received Rs. 5,65,000.[17]

The big Gujarati merchants of Bombay operated and made money chiefly as agents of British merchant capital and so obtained bulk of their profits. At the same time, the early seats of industrial enterprise appeared in Bombay. Upto the end of the 18th century, the British energetically implanted handloom weaving in Bombay, as they did in other factories throughout India. In November 1678, a letter was sent from the Surat factory to Bombay recommending that weavers from Surat should be invited to Bombay to manufacture calicoes. The letter expressed the confidence that the invitation would be accepted by the weavers who had suffered from the consequences of the Maratha wars. By 1676, a regular industry had been established in Bombay. The Company imported raw silk and cotton and distributed it to the weavers who worked under a Muquadam and were paid partly in money and partly in rice.[18]

The Gazetteer of Bombay City and Island gives information on the handicrafts in Bombay during the 17th and 18th centuries. These documents help us to form an opinion of the duties which the Indian middlemen, called Muquadam, performed. The documents of the Bombay Council of the East India Company show that in the 1730s the resettlement of the weavers in Bombay was preceded by negotiations in which the Muquadam put forward, on their behalf, a number of demands on the building of houses, supply of raw materials etc.Through the Muquadam the Company recruited weavers, supplied them with raw materials, advanced money to them, collected the finished products and paid the weavers in cash and food stuffs.The trust which the British placed in their agents was extremely great, for at those times sums amounting to several thousands of rupees passed through their hands for which they did not have to account. The agent was only obliged to handover a fixed quantity of manufactured goods. Since the weavers completely depended upon the Muquadams, the agent was able to exploit them in his own interest. Several Muquadams are mentioned by name in various documents. At the beginning of the 18th century, the Chief Master of the weavers working for the East India Company in Bombay was a Parsi named Manek.[19]

The need of European market was catered by the handloom weaving in Bombay. In 1670, the Company even sent English weavers, dyers and other artisans to India to show the Indians how to manufacture the goods which were most likely to find favour with the Europeans and which would therefore prove to be most profitable for the Company. From 1724 to 1725, Cawasji Rustomji was in England with his family from where he brought back 12 tin pipe-coils and three stills for the making of alcoholic drinks. R. V. Wadia and D. Dadiseth were the first to use wine making presses in the 1780s.

However, it was shipbuilding enterprise in Bombay that outclassed all capitalistic efforts. The shipyard in Bombay was set up by the East India Company in 1730. In 1735, Lowji Nusurwanji Wadia was invited from Surat dockyard to Bombay where he worked as a shipwright. He was the ancestor of the Wadia family from which came many leading shipbuilders of Bombay and later on at the end of the 19th century, a number of mill owners. The good quality of the vessels built in Bombay dockyard can be ascertained by looking at a letter written by the Chief Officer of a Bombay frigate to its builder, Jamshetji Baharamji. The letter stated that a fleet of 17 British ships spent the winter of 1808-1809 in extremely difficult ice conditions in the Baltic Sea and that only the frigate which was built in bombay escaped serious damage.[20] The brilliant history of such a shipbuilding industry ended when British capitalists took up direct control over India after the abolition of East India Company in 1857. The closer of Bombay shipbuilding was not just because of economic considerations, as the ships built in Bombay were much cheaper, in fact the British government wanted to deprive India of her shipbuilding facilities, and intruded to establish a British monopoly of maritime transport. The British capitalists succeeded very much in their attempt. The Bombay shipbuilding activity would have developed into a full-fledged industry, had India been free at that time.

By the first half of the 19th century, the Gujarati merchants (Parsis, Bhatia, Memons, Bohras, and Jains) collaborated with British in the growth of industrial capital. The field in which this collaboration existed included broking in commercial transactions, export of opium, credit operations, shipbuilding and other industries in Bombay. The Bombay merchants had a very firm and cordial relations with the British only and because of this relation, they were able to build industrial enterprises earlier than those in other parts of country and the fact is that this also led to the straining of their relations subsequently with them.

The big Gujarati merchants collaborated with the British capitalists in order to gain accumulation of their capital. They succeeded in their ventures through their mercantile activities in cotton and opium as well as shipbuilding industry. They amassed a good deal of wealth too. But in the first half of the 19th century, they could not play any leading role in the capitalistic enterprises because, although they were numerically stronger in number than the Europeans, the native merchant capital remained subordinated to the British industrial capital. It was true that some of the Parsis did invest in shipbuilding activity where they had the potential to grow but the Europeans closed down the industry by 1857 as they found the native merchants as great rivals to them.

However, the Marwaris, who operated mainly as moneylenders, were not at all interested in investing in the capitalist enterprises. They remained confined to their usarious business. Although they utilized the colonial conditions to their fullest possible advantage for amassing wealth, they remained reluctant in their investment for capitalistic development. Hence, their capital did not play any major role till the end of the nineteenth century. As early as 1676, regular hand industry was established in Bombay and by the close of the seventeenth century Bombay island witnessed some more entrepreneurial activities like manufacture of knitted stockings in 1683, gunpowder in 1677, Bidi making, carriage-making, basket making, hookka making and leaf fan making, etc. The first attempt to set up a textile mill along the capitalist line was made by Dr. Bhau Daji who mooted a proposal to set up textile mill in Bombay in 1851.[21] After four years, Cawasji Nanabhai Davar floated the first textile mill in 1854.

During the second half of the nineteenth century, British capital got very firmly deep rooted in Bombay. The raw-materials were exported to England either via Bombay or Calcutta. The only difference between the two cities was that Calcutta exported jute while Bombay exported cotton. Another point of difference in both the cities was that Calcutta was directly developed by the British firms while Bombay came to be developed by means of independent native capital. Consequently, independent capitalist development took place relatively later in Calcutta than Bombay where the resistance of freedom loving Marathas forced the British to give greater independence to native wealthy classes for their collaboration.

Thus, Bombay developed as the centre of national capitalist economy under the most favourable condition that existed for the collaboration with British capital. And it became chiefly responsible for the building up of cotton mills by the Gujarati big merchants of Bombay in collaboration with the British capitalists. As a result of this development the first group of the national capitalists emerged in the personalities like Dadabhoy Nawroji, Pherozshah Mehta and M. G. Ranade. Thus, the heroic resistance by the Marathas against colonialists benefited the natives in two ways. *Firstly,* it enriched the patriotic traditions of the people and *secondly,* it lead to the appearance of the conditions in which new classes of Indian society emerged.

In the year 1919, the Indian Industrial Commission reported that most of the capital invested in the cotton mills of Bombay consisted of profits derived from the opium export to China, and off course, from the gains which the cotton boom brought to Bombay in the 1860s.[22] The capital required for the building of textile mills was acquired from the trade in opium, cotton and British textile while acting in collaboration with the English capitalists. Thus, was laid the foundation for the large scale factory system of industry in India by the emerging capitalists of Bombay. It should be kept in mind that the British capitalists began to construct Jute mill at Calcutta two years later. This fact is a clear proof that Bombay merchants were better prepared to undertake industrial ventures than other groups of Indian traders and they preferred investing their capital into large scale industry rather than investing in the commercial and money lending fields. Bombay merchants could take up the industrial ventures because they had well learnt from their collaborations with English capitalists about the risks involved in the capital investment in modern industry.

The first Company for the building of a cotton spinning mill in Bombay was set up in 1851 and began to work on 5th February 1854. Its equipments were supplied by a British firm, 'Platt Brothers and Company of Oldham' which became the principal supplier of machinery for the factories built later in Bombay.[23] Cawasji Nanabhoy Davar was the promoter of the company who floated the first Textile Mill in 1854 and opened another spinning mill in 1857.

'The Oriental' was the first weaving mill that began operating from 1860 and whose Directors were a Parsi and a Hindu who came from Kapol Bania community. Some members of Bhatia community also ventured into the industrial enterprises. The most prominent among them was Keshavji Naik who started a weaving mill 'Royal' and Morarji Gokuldas who established 'The Great Eastern Mill'. In 1860 itself a member of Kapol Bania community named Nathubhai Mangaldas began operating the sixth enterprise in Bombay.

Thus, by the end of 1860, there were nine factories in Bombay but the outbreak of the Civil War in America changed the situation as the native merchants of Bombay got indulged in speculative business to earn quick profit. As a result of this, the process of building factories came to be delayed and in place of that the joint stock companies, banks and finance corporations came to be floated, with a view to invest more in cotton for getting more and quick profit.[24] In other words, the high prices of cotton led to its export rather than to feed the local industry that needed cheap cotton. This led to a slack period in the development of local industries.

After the end of the Civil War, the situation again improved and the second generation of Bombay industrialists arose from amongst the rank of cotton dealers. Among the big capitalists of the nineteen sixtees were the Parsi P. R. Kolah and the first Muslim mill owner Kasumbhoy Dharmsay who was a Gujarati Khoja Muslim and a trader. Both these persons were well known cotton merchants. Kasumbhoy Dharmsay remained engaged in his commercial transactions in cooperation with the British even after becoming a mill owner and was considered to be one of the richest men in India.[25]

Among the native capitalists of the latter half of the 19th century, the most prominent personality was of Jamshedji Nusservanji Tata, a Parsi. He built-up the cotton mill 'Alexandra' in Bombay in the year 1869 but sold it in 1871 to Keshavji Naik for opening 'Empress Mill' in Nagpur and the new mill began operating in the month of January, 1877. It gave enormous profit to him enabling him to accumulate vast capital with which later on he built-up Iron and Steel Works and Hydro-Electric Power Station.

Among the member of the Bhatia community names of Gokuldas Tejpal and Sunderlal Jaitha is worth mentioning. They rose to be mill owners from the rank of cotton merchants who collaborated with British. Another member of this community was Thakersey Moolji who also became a manufacturer in 1873 from the rank of being a cotton merchant. However, it should not be presumed that these capitalists were only from the ranks of merchants dealing in cotton. Even the merchant who acted as middlemen to the English in other commercial activities also became the manufacturers.

Among other capitalists of 70s, who were the owners of mills were Petit, Ahmed Habibbhoy, Ardeshir H. Wadia, Burjorji R. Mody and Sassoons who all started mills as a result of which the number of mills rose to eleven by 1874. But the fact is that the developing large scale industry in Bombay was completely dependent on Britain for the supply of machinery for the factories. The colonial regime obstructed the creation of machine-building industry thereby delaying the industrial development. This also made the native industrialist to depend on the British capital. Consequently, the British Capitalists were forced to 'collaborate' with native industrialists on unfavourable terms.

After 1874, once again the slack period followed in the industrial activity of Bombay. Between 1874 to 1882 only two industrial enterprises were built in Bombay. The factory owners were Premchand Roychand and Manmohandas Ramji. Premchand Roychand was the biggest speculator in landed property and a partner of Tata while Manmohandas Ramji traded in British textiles and represented the Ralli Brothers, the leading Cotton Export Company.[26]

The year 1883 was the record year in the history of cotton industry in Bombay when it saw the birth of as many as 13 mills. Five of these mills were owned by British firms Greaves, Cotton and Co., while three other mills came to be founded by other British Companies including Sassoons. In 1883, the British capital made its entry in the cotton industry of Bombay and did not allow the small native capitalist to establish independent industrial enterprises.

However, in all 57 new enterprises came to be started in Bombay between 1881 to 1900 out of which 18 mills were built by British capitalists including Sassoons. During the period of 20 years from 1881 to 1900 the participation of British capital in the building of industrial enterprises was at its peak because before 1880 the British had built 3 mills and after 1900 just one mill. By 1895, fourteen of the seventy mills operating in Bombay were directly controlled by British capitalists.[27]

In the beginning of the 20th century, the big Indian capitalist of Bombay mainly consisted of Gujaratis although strong group of Marwari capitalists also began to emerge. Commerce in Bombay remained to a considerable extent in the hands of the people who spoke Gujarati and were the local traders. Writing about the Bombay Port, W. Digby remarked that a sufficient large amount of capital circulated in Bombay satisfying all the requirements of the great port city. Greater part of the capital belonged to foreigners, European merchants (other than English). Bulk of the indigenous capital did not come from local sources either but belonged to Indian bankers and merchants from the native principalities, who owned approximately Rs. 60 million of the capital that circulated in Bombay. As an important group of rich merchants who had more or less settled down in Bombay were emigrants from the native states.[28]

In 1900, the capitalist class in Bombay was comprised of the modern class of capitalist who came from industrial, commercial and financial as well as the professional classes such as doctors, lawyers and high government officers. The capitalists who were the industrialist began to rise from a microscopic community of Parsis which was later on joined by some member of some Hindu trading castes of Bania, Bhatia, Jain, Marwari etc., [29] and a few individuals of Baghdadi Jewish community and also European community by the middle of 1850s in the city. Some individuals who emerged as Indian Industrial bourgeoisie were Cawasji Nanabhai Davar, Maneckji Nasservanji Petit, D. M. Petit, Jahangir Modi, Ardeshir H. Wadia, Nanabhoy B. Jijibhoy, Mancherji H. Banaji, Hormusji Bataliwala, Nusserwanji Wadia, Nusserwanji Katruck, Jamshed Tata, Keshavji Naik, Morarji Gokuldas, Dwarkadas Vasanji, Moolji Jaitha, Jadhavji Raghoji, Thackersey Mulji, Khatau Makanji, Mangaldas Nathubhai, Jivraj Balloo, Tejpal Heerji, K. M. Heera Maneckji, Lukshmidas Kheemji, Essa Khalifa, Dhurmsay Punjabhai, Ahamadbhai Habibbhai,

Elias Sassoon. James Greaves, James Latimar & Co., James Dunkerley, Killick Nixon & Company, Kettle Well Bullen & Co., Shaw Wallace & Co., etc. were of the European origin. The Bhatias were chiefly cloth merchants, landlords and mill owners.[30] The Jains were bankers, jewelers, Shroffs and commission agents.[31] The Marwari's were moneylenders.[32] The Khojas were landlords, mill owners, general merchants, contractors and did a large trade in imports and exports. The Bohras and Memons were landlords, contractors, stationary, merchants and general traders.[33] The Parsis were spectacularly present in every branch of trade. The European capitalists were usually large importers and exporters while many Hindu and Jain capitalists were stock and share brokers. The Marwari's made profit by investing in money lending and banking though some of them invested their wealth in mill shares and house property and a few invested their capital in ginning and pressing factories.[34] the Jains and Bhatias cared little for governmental securities, bank shares, and purchased immovable properties. The Banias of Cutch invested their savings in business only, while the Khojas purchased the shares of joint stock companies and Municipal Port Trust and City Improvement Trust Bonds.[35] The only Maratha, mentioned by Gazetteer of Bombay City and Island, were the Brahmins from Deccan, listed among the castes that have produced some of the wealthy inhabitants of Bombay. Since there were no businessmen among the Brahmins at that time one can assume that the wealthy Marathas were either land owners, who lived in Bombay, or prosperous members of the free professions, particularly lawyers.

The nature of the growth of commercial capitalist from the middle of the 19th century indicates how European capitalists had surpassed Indians capitalists by 1875. In 1850, there were about 431 foreign exporters, 228 Indians and 203 Europeans. Of these traders about 16 Indians and only 6 Europeans were the leading one. In 1861, the total number of exporters in the city was 548, of which 505 were Indians and 43 Europeans, the topmost being only 12 Indians and 5 Europeans. So far Indians were concerned; they were in the lead in the foreign trade.[36] But by 1875, the Europeans surpassed the Indians in trade, as in 1875 of the 379 Indian traders only 3 were the leading traders and of the 42 European traders as many as 21 were leading traders.[37] The Indian commercial capitalist gradually became very critical of the British government for its preferential treatment to European business and undue restrictions on Indian trade with non-British countries.[38]

In 1900-1901, the total population of the city was 7,76,006 of which 5,00,868 were Hindus, 1,55,747 were Muslims, 45,176 were Christians and the rest were others. Of the 45,176 Christians only 15,531 were Europeans and Eurasians. It seems that the number of Europeans was not more than 10,000. Of this population of slightly over 7½ lakhs those who can be called capitalist in general were 18,849 because they were assessed as income taxpayers. Of these people about 1/3 were owners of share holders in companies, big traders, property owners etc. The table on next page shows the various sources of taxpayers at the end of the 19th century.[39]

Sources of Income	*Number of Assesses*	
	At 4 Pice per Rupees	*At 5 Pice per Rupees*
Part I: Salaries & C.	5,824	2,365
Total I	5,824	2,365
Part II: Companies		
Banking	...	006
Building and land	...	004
Cotton spinning and weaving	...	070
Cotton pressing, ginning and cleaning	...	053
Flour mills	...	003
Insurance fire, life marine	...	035
Printing & Publishing	...	002
Steam Navigation	...	002
Railways	...	007

Telegraph & Telephone ...	003
Tramway ...	002
Other ...	057
Total II	244

Part IV : Other Sources

Sources of Income	Number of Assesses	
	At 4 Pice per Rupees	At 5 Pice per Rupees
(a) Procession	...	...
Education	024	004
Engineering and Architecture	024	029
Law-Barristers	014	042
Law-attorneys, pleaders and Other Practitioners	056	073
Medical	107	084
Others	112	064
Total (a)	337	296
(b) Manufacture, construction and manipulation (other than companies cotton spinning and weaving)	001	007
Flour Mills	001	004
Metal works	017	010
Oil Mills	002	002
Rope works	005	004
Saw and Timber Mill	001	002
Silk reding and weaving	005	004
Spirits	005	006
Sugar making & refining	007	009
Tanneries & leather work	002	001
Others	153	058
Total (b)	194	104

Sources of Income	*Number of Assesses*	
	At 4 Pice per Rupees	*At 5 Pice per Rupees*
(c) Commerce and trade agents and brokers	679	626
Bankers & Money lenders	725	232
Contractors	049	052
Merchants and dealers in:-		
(i) Animals, including stable keepers	007	015
(ii) Apparel and drapery	046	021
(iii) Books and materials	029	020
(iv) Building materials	062	028
(v) Food grains	356	062
(vi) Other food stuffs (Grocer and provisions)	145	048
(vii) Hides and skins	015	013
(viii) Liquor	148	029
(ix) Metal (other than gold & silver)	044	038
(x) Opium	004	014
(xi) Piece goods (cotton, wool, silk)	479	287
(xii) Precious stone and jewellery	036	051
(xiii) Salt	003	005
(xiv) Other commodities	031	014
Total (c)	3,829	2,098
(d) Property owners of: Houses	1,751	1,518
Estates Taxable under the Act	0020	0017
Total (d)	1,771	1,535
(e) Others not classified above	0195	0057
Total (e)	0195	0057
Total (IV)	6,326	4,090
Grand Total	12,150	6,699
Grand Total	(18,849)	

By 1900, the top most capitalists in Bombay were Europeans, generally traders and industrialists. As for instance, the top most capitalist making more than a lakhs of rupees as profit were 74 of which 35 made money from Joint Stock Company and 39 from other sources. Among these capitalists, majority were Europeans. As for instance, from amongst 39 capitalists who made their income from trade and professions only 7 were Hindu mill owners, 6 Parsi merchants and brokers and 4 Muslims. It implied that in the top group of capitalists only 17 were natives while 22 were Europeans, generally merchants and industrialists.

The following Table shows the number of tax payers by classes of income in Bombay by the end of the 19th century.[40]

Class of Income		*Number of Assesser*		
		Salaries Pensions Etc.	*Profits of Joint Stock Companies*	*Other Sources of Income*
(i)	Rs. 1,000 but less than Rs. 1,250	3,638	007	3,237
(ii)	Rs. 1,250 but less than Rs. 1,500	0678	003	1,047
(iii)	Rs. 1,500 but less than Rs. 1,750	0579	002	0899
(iv)	Rs. 1,750 but less than Rs. 2,000	0929	003	0783
Total of Classes I to IV		5,824	015	6,326
(v)	Rs. 2,000 but less than Rs. 2,500	0667	007	0956
(vi)	Rs. 2,500 but less than Rs. 5,000	1,190	026	1,546
(vii)	Rs. 5,000 but less than Rs. 10,000	0384	046	0844
(viii)	Rs. 10,000 but less than Rs. 20,000	0104	041	0417
(ix)	Rs. 20,000 but less than Rs. 30,000	0017	030	0144
(x)	Rs. 30,000 but less than Rs. 40,000	0003	011	0072
(xi)	Rs. 40,000 but less than Rs. 50,000	—	012	0023
(xii)	Rs. 50,000 but less than Rs. 1,00,000	—	021	0049
(xiii)	Rs. 1,00,000 and above	—	035	039
Total of Classes V to XIII		2,365	229	4,090

An analysis of the given Table indicates that the small capitalists making an annual income between Rs. 20,000 to Rs. 30,000 were 191, of these 17 were salaried persons, 30 belonged to the group who made profit out of joint stock company and 144 were agents, brokers, property owners, cloth merchants etc. In this category of 191 capital owners, and cloth merchants, 20 were European barristers, merchants and agents, 23 were Parsi merchants and 29 were Khoja, Memon and Bohra property owners and general merchants. In the same way the number of capitalists whose annual income was between Rs. 30,000 to Rs. 40,000 were 86, of these 36 were Hindus, 15 were Musalmans, 11 were Parsis, 10 were Europeans. Similarly, out of 35 capitalists having annual income between Rs. 40,000 to Rs, 50,000, 9 were Parsis, 8 were Hindus, 4 were Europeans, and 8 were Musalmans, while out of 70 capitalists whose annual income went from Rs. 50,000 to Rs. 1,00,000, 15 were Hindu agents, 13 were Parsi landlords, 12 were European merchants and 9 were Mohammadan general merchants. In the top most categories were 74 capitalists with annual income over Rs. 1,00,000. Among them the Europeans, as stated earlier, dominated having the strength more than double the strength of the Indian capitalists. The above analysis shows that in the lower income group of capitalists the Europeans were a few but in the higher income group the number of European capitalist was very large.[41]

Thus, in the light of the above discussion it has become crystal clear that even by the end of the 19th century the Europeans dominated the economic scene of Bombay and the native capitalists failed in surpassing them. However, strong resistance to the British colonial rule did appear from emerging intelligentia who were the products of Western education. This newly emerged class became responsible for showing to the people the real nature of the English ruling class and prepared the background for freedom struggle not only in Bombay but the whole country. On one hand, the intelligentia opposed the imperialist economy and on the other they advocated the development of indigenous capitalism by promoting nationalistic outlooks.

The intellectuals and the business class came closer to each other as the British government became their common enemy and perhaps this was the reason why the Indian National Congress became the rallying ground for both. This is proved from the fact that in Poona Session of Indian National Congress in 1895, 437 members of the commercial class participated while the total number of delegates attending the Congress was 1,584.[42]

Men like Dadabhoy Nawroji and G. K. Gokhale were not businessmen but they agitated for the development of indigenous capitalistic enterprise. They believed that the operation of the imperialist economy obstructed the pace of industrial progress, though it encouraged agricultural and commercial development. The dominance of the import industry had the effect of destroying the country's artisan's production without promoting a corresponding increase in the output of textile goods. The paucity of indigenous capital, technical skill, and enterprises purely accounted for the state of industrial backwardness. M. N. Roy also wrote that "Economic necessities forced the intellectual bourgeoisies to begin its political struggle, which was initiated in the form of Indian National Congress, whose first session was held in 1885 in Bombay, under the Presidency of W. C. Bannerji, a rich lawyer who had his savings invested in commercial and industrial enterprise. The object of this political movement was to replace or at least to curtail the power of the British Government, which was standing in the way of economic development of the bourgeoisie. This movement was headed by rich lawyers, merchants, mill owners, physicians etc., or in other words, that progressive element of the society which possessed capital to be invested."[43] He further commented that "The economic power of the Indian bourgeoisie, composed of the intellectuals, mercantile capitalists, liberal land holders, and the industrial capitalists, had acquired sufficient strength to enable it to declare an open struggle against the foreign capitalistic monopoly."[44]

The British administrators realized their mistake of creating an educated class of Indians who started demanding an equal share in the administration of their country. This was the reason why the British administration tried to retard the progress of higher education by promoting primary education and limiting the responsibility of state in education.

REFERENCES

1. S. M. Edwardes: *The Rise of Bombay*, p. 107.
2. *Ibid.*
3. *Gazetteer of Bombay Presidency, (Ahmadabad)*, Vol. IV, p. 89. (Hereafter to be referred as G.B.P.)
4. *Ibid.*, p. 90.
5. *G.B.P.*, Vol. XXVI *(Materials of Bombay), Pt. I, 'History' Bombay,* 1893, p. 46.
6. *Ibid., Pt. – I, "Trade and Fortifications" Bombay, 1894*, p. 208.
7. *G.B.P. (Bombay)*, 1909, Vol. I, pp. 152, 154.
8. S. M. Edwardes: *The Rise of Bombay*, p. 136.
9. CH. Fawcett: *English Factories in India (Oxford 1936)*, Vol. I, p. 79.
10. *G.B.P.*, Vol. I, p. 414.
11. W. Hamilton: *East India Gazetteer (London 1828)*, Vol. I, p. 261.
12. J. Forbes: *Oriental Memoires*, Vol. II, p. 56.
13. J. Douglas: *Bombay under Western India, Vol. I*, pp. 241-242.
14. J. M. Maclean: *A Guide to Bombay-Historical, Statistical and Descriptive (Bombay 1880)*, p. 105.
15. W. H. Coates: *The Old Country Trade (London, 1911)*, pp. 51, 90.
16. J. Burnell: *Bombay in the days of Queen Anne (London 1933)*, p. 110.
17. *G.B.P., Pt. I (Gujarat Population Hindus), Bombay, 1899*, Vol. IX, p. 196
18. *G.B.C.I. (Bombay, 1909)*, Vol. I, p. 462.
19. Ch. Fawcett: *Op.cit.*, Vol. I, p. 57.
20. C. R. Low: *History of the Indian Navy (London, 1877)*, Vol – I, pp. 278, 298.
21. S. D. Mehta: *Indian Cotton Textile Industry, 1854-1954*, p. 7.
22. *Indian Industrial Commission Report (London, 1919) I*, p. 65.

23. S. M. Rutnagur: *The Bombay Industries, The Cotton Mills*, p. 9.
24. *Imperial Gazetteer of India*, Vol. II, p. 211.
25. *Indian Textile Journal (July, 1934).*
26. C. H. Rao: *Indian Biographical Dictionary*, p. 34.
27. *Ibid.*, p. 137.
28. W. Digby: *Prosperous British India*, p. 185.
29. G.B.C.I. (1909), Vol. I, p. 293.
30. *Ibid.*
31. *Ibid.*
32. *Ibid.*
33. *Ibid.*
34. *Ibid.*, p. 294.
35. *Ibid.*
36. Marika Vicziany: *'Bombay Merchants Structural Change in Export Community 1850-1880' in Economy and Society edited by* K. N. Chowdhari & C.J. Dewey, (O.U.P. 1979), pp. 163-188.
37. *Ibid.*
38. A. R. Desai: *Social Background of Indian Nationalism (Bombay, II Edition, 1954)*, p. 201.
39. G.B.C.I., Vol. I, pp. 332-334.
40. *Ibid.*, p. 294.
41. *Ibid. (An analysis by the researcher).*
42. B. B. Misra: *The Indian Middle Classes*, p. 357.
43. M. N. Roy: *India in Transition (1917)*, p. 27.
44. *Ibid.*, p. 27.

BIBLIOGRAPHY

Manuscripts

Government of Maharashtra Secretariat Record office, Elphinston College Building, Mumbai.

The following volumes from 1820 to 1900 have been referred :

(i) Files of General Administration Department.

(ii) Files of Finance Department.

(iii) Files of Judicial Department.

(iv) Files of Revenue Department.

(v) Files of Political Department.

(vi) Files of Education Department.

(vii) Public Department Letters from the East India Company to Surat and Bombay (1618-1685); one volume.

PUBLISHED WORKS

Danvers, F. C. : Report to the Secretary of State for India in Council on the Portuguese Records relating to the East Indies, London, 1892.

Fawcett, C. (ed.) : The English Factories in India 1670-77. Vol. I, Oxford, 1936 and Vol. II, (1678-1784). Oxford, 1954.

Forrest, G. W. : Selections from the Letters, Dispatches and Other State Papers, preserved in Bombay Secretariat, Home Series, Vol. I & II, Bombay, 1887.

Forrest, G. W. : Selections from the Letters, Dispatches and Other State Papers, Maratha Series, Vol. I, Bombay, 1885.

Forrest, G.W. : Selections from the State Papers, East India Company's Connections with the Persian Gulf with a Summary of Events, 1600-1800, London, 1906.

Khan, S.A. : Anglo-Portuguese Negotiations Relating to Bombay (1660-67) Oxford, 1922.

Khan, S.A. : Documents on XVIIth Century British India, London, 1924.

Khan, S.A. : Sources of the History of British India in the Seventeenth Century, London, 1926.

Leith, A. H. : Census of the Island of Bombay taken on Second February, 1864, Bombay, 1864.

Saensbury, E.E. & Foster, W. (ed) : A Calendar of Court Minutes etc. of the East India Company 1635-79, 2 Vols. Oxford, 1907-38.

ADMINISTRATIVE REPORTS AND PROCEEDINGS

Proceedings of the Bombay Legislative Council, 1862-1939.

Bombay Native Newspapers Reports, 9 Vols.

Memorandum on the Material Condition of the People of Bombay Presidency, 1881-1892.

Statement Showing the Moral and Material Progress of India, 1866-67.

A Review of Education in Bombay State 1855-1955, Poona, 1958.

CENSUS REPORTS

Census of the Island of Bombay, 1864.

Imperial Census of India, Bombay City Part, 1871.

Census of India, Bombay City Part, 1881.

Census of India, Bombay City Part, 1891.

Census of India, Bombay City Part, 1901.

GAZETTEERS

Gazetteer of Bombay Presidency, Vols. I, II, IV, IX to XIII, XV and XVII (1877-96).

Imperial Gazetteer of India, Vol. II, III, 1908. Vol- IV, 1909 (Oxford).

J.M. Campbell : Gazetteer of Bombay Presidency, Material towards a Statistical Account of Town and Island of Bombay, 3 Vols.

S.M. Edwardes : Gazetteer of Bombay City and Island, 3 Vols, Bombay, 1909-10.

K.K.Chowdhari (ed) : Gazetteer of India, Maharashtra State Gazetteer, Greater Bombay District: Bombay, 1986, 3 Vols.

Thorton Edwards : Gazetteer of the Territories under the Government of East India Company, London, 1857.

NON-GOVERNMENT SOURCES

Annual Reports of Bombay Chamber of Commerce, 1840 onwards.

Annual Reports of Bombay Mill Owners Association (1877-1950).

Minutes and Proceedings of the Bombay Association 1852, 1855 and 1873.

NEWSPAPERS AND PERIODICALS

Bombay Courier	1830-1845
The Bombay Gazetteer	1840-1930
Bombay Times	1840-1860
The Bombay Chronicle	Stray Copies
Rast Goftar	Stray Copies
Indu Prakash	Stray Copies
The Bombay Samachar	Stray Copies
The Native Opinion	Stray Copies

Journal of the Bombay Branch of Asiatic Society

The Social and Economic History Review.

Bombay Quarterly Review.

Economic and Political Weekly.

Economic Weekly, Bombay.

Proceeding Volumes of Indian History Congress.

TRAVELOGES

Forbes, James : Oriental Memoirs. A Narrative of Seventeen Years Residence in India, Vol-I, London, 1834.

Fryer, John : A New Account of East India and Persia, Vol. I, II & III, London, 1915.

Hamilton, A. : A New Account of East India, Vol. I, London, 1930.

Ovington, James : A Voyage to Surat in the year 1689, (Ed.) H. G. Rawlinson, Oxford, 1929.

Temples R. C. : The Diaries of Streynsham Master, 2 Vols, London, 1911.

OTHER SOURCES

Acharya, B.P. and Shingne, M.V. : Mumbaiche Vritant, Marathi (Bombay, 1887).

Acharya, Hemlata : 'Creative Response in Indian Economy, A Comment' in 'Economic Weekly', Bombay IX (April 17, 1957).

Anderson, Philip : The English in Western India (London, 1886).

Anon : Representative Men of the Bombay Presidency (U.S.A. 1900).

Anon : A Collection of Obituary and other Notices Illustrative of the Life of the Late Honourable Jagannath Shankar Shet (Bombay, 1867).

Arnold, Edwin : India Revisited (London, 1886).

Anstey, Veera : Economic development of India (London, 1949).

Bagchi, A.K. : Private Investment in India, 1900 to 1939 (Cambridge, 1972).

Bagchi, A.K. : 'European and Indian Entrepreneurship in India: 1900-1930,' in E. Leach and S. N. Mukharjee (ed) Elites in South Asia (Cambridge, England...).

Bagchi, A.K. : Capital and Labour Re defined – India and the third world (New Delhi, 2002).

Baran Paul, A : The Political Economy of Growth, Indian Edition (New Delhi, 1917).

Basu, D : Rise and Growth of Colonial Port Cities of Asia (Berkely, 1985).

Benden-Powell, B. H. : A Short Account of Land Revenue and its administration in British India, with a Sketch of Land Tenures (Oxford, 1894).

Buchanan, F : A Journey from Madras (London, 1804).

Burchanan, D.H. : The Development of Capitalistic Enterprise in India (New York, 1934).

Burnell, J. : Bombay in the Days of Queen Anne (London, 1933).

Bhargava : Indigenous Banking in Ancient and Medieval India (Bombay, 1934).

Briggs, G. : The Cities of Gujarashtra (Bombay, 1840).

Briggs, G. : The Parsis of Modern Zerdusthians: A Sketch (Edinburg, 1852).

Campbell, J.M. : Material Towards a Stastical Account of the Town and Island of Bombay, 3 Vols. (Bombay, 1893-94).

Chandavarkar, R. : The Origins of Industrial Capitalism in India (New Delhi, 1994).

Chandra, Bipin : Rise and Growth of Economic Nationalism in India (New Delhi, 1964).

Chapman, J. : The Cotton and Commerce of India (London, 1860).

Chowdhari, K.N. : "Market and Traders in India during the Seventeenth and Eighteenth Centuries," in K.N. Chowdhari and C. J. Devey (Ed.) Economy and Society. Essays in Indian Economic and Social History (O.U.P., New Delhi, 1979).

Chowdhari, K.N. : "Foreign Trade and Balance of Payments, 1757-1957," in Dharmakumar and Tapan Raychaudhari (ed.) Cambridge Economic History of India, Vol. II (Cambridge University Press, London, 1883).

Charlesworth, Nell : British Rule and the Indian Economy, 1800-1900 (London, 1982).

Chintamani, C.Y. (ed.) : Speeches and writings of the Honourable Sir Pherozshah Mehta (Allahabad, 1905).

Chintamani, C.Y. : Indian Politics since the Mutiny (Allahabad, 1917).

Chinoy, S. Chisney : Pioneering in Indian Business (New York, 1962).

General George : Indian Polity (3rd edition, London, 1904).

Choksey, R.D. : Economic History of Bombay, Deccan and Karnataka (1818-1868). (Poona, 1945).

Choksey, R.D. : Economic Life in the Bombay, Deccan (1818-1939), (Bombay, 1955).

Claridge, G. : Old and New Bombay (Bombay, 1911).

Coates, W.H. : The Old Country Trade (London, 1911).

Davy, Brian : Economic Development of India (London, 1975).

David, M.D. : History of Bombay 1661-1708 (Bombay University, 1973) Published Thesis.

David, M.D. : Bombay: The City of Dreams (A history of the first city in India) (Bombay, 1995).

Dagobert, D. Runner (ed.) : The Dictionary of Philosophy (New York, 1942).

Darryal, D'monte : Ripping in Fabrics – The Decline of Mumbai and its Mills (Delhi, O.U.P. 2002).

Darukhandwala, H. D. : Parsi Lusture on Indian Soil (Bombay, 1939).

Daruwala, R : The Bombay Chamber Story: 150 years (Bombay, 1986).

D'Cunha, J.G. : The Origins of Bombay (Bombay, 1900).

Desai, Ashok V. : "The Origins of Parsi Enterprise : The Indian Economic and Social History Review, Dec. 1968.

Dighe. V. G. : 'The Renaissance in Maharashtra, First phase (1818-70)' in Journal of the Asiatic Society of Bombay, Vol. 36-7, 1961-2.

Digby, William : Prosperous British India (London, 1901).

Dobbin, Christine : Urban Leadership in Western India: Politics and Communities in Bombay, 1840-85 (Bombay, 1972).

Dobbin, Christine : 'Competing Elites in Bombay City in Nineteenth Century' in Leach, E.R. and Mukharjee S.N. (ed.) Elites in South Asia (Cambridge, 1970).

Dongerkery, S.R. : A History of the University of Bombay (1857-1957) (University of Bombay, 1957).

Douglas, J. : Bombay and Western India, 2 Vols (London, 1893).

Douglas, J. : English and Native Rule in India (Bombay, 1868).

Douglas, J. : A Book of Bombay (Bombay, 1883).

Dutta, R.C. : The Economic History of India Vol. II: In the Victorian Age, 1857-1900 (Delhi, 1960).

Dumasia, N. : A Short Biographical Sketch of Late Sheth Varjeevandas Madhovdas (Bombay, 1896).

Eckchard Kulcke : The Parsis in India (Delhi, 1978).

Edwardes, S.M. : The Rise of Bombay: A Retrospect (B'bay, 1902).

Fawcett, C.H. : English Factories in India (Oxford, 1936).

Forbes, James : Oriental Memoirs–A Narrative of Seventeen Years Residence in India (London, 1834).

Forbes, A.K. : Rasmala, Hindoo Annals of the provinces of Goozerat in Western India II (London, 1856).

Fryer, J. : A New Account of East India and Persia, Vol. I.

Gadgil, D.R. : Origins of Modern Indian Business Class. An Interim Report (unpublished) (New York, 1959).

Gadgil, D.R. : Industrial Evolution of India in Recent Times (4th edition, Calcutta, 1948).

Gadgil, D.R. : Notes on the Rise of Business Communities in India (New York, 1951).

Gillion, K. I. : Ahmedabad: A study in Urban History (Berkley, Calif, 1969).

Ghose. S.K. : The Indian Big Bourgeoisies. It's Genesis Growth and Character (Calcutta, 1985).

Graham, Maria : Journal of the Residence in India (Edinburg, 1813).

Gordon, A.D.D. : Businessmen and Politics: Rising Nationalism and a Modernizing Economy in Bombay, 1918 to 1933 (New Delhi, 1978).

Gordon, Johnson : Provincial Politics and Indian Nationalism: Bombay and the Indian National Congress, 1880-1915 (Cambridge, 1973).

Gopalkrishna, D.K. : Development of Economic Ideas in India: 1880-1950 (New Delhi, 1959).

Gupta, J.N. : Life and work of Romesh Chander Dutta (London, 1911).

Guha, Amlendu : 'The Comprador Role of Parsi Sethia, 1750-1850' in 'Economic and Political' Weekly, dated November 28, 1970.

Guha, Amlendu : 'More About Parsi Seths—Their Roots, Entrepreneurship and Comprador Role: 1650-1915' in Tripathi Dwijendra (ed.) Business Communities of India: A Historical Perspective (New Delhi, 1984).

Hamilton, C. J. : The Trade Relations Between England And India, 1600-1806 (Calcutta, 1919).

Hamilton, Jenks, Leland : The Migration of British Capital to 1875 (New York, 1927).

Hamilton, A. : A New Account of the East Indies, Vol. I (London, 1930).

Hamilton, W. : East India Gazetteer (London, 1828).

Haris, F. : Jamshedji Nasserwanjee Tata: A Chronicle of his Life (Bombay, 1958).

Haris, F.H. : The Life of J.N.Tata (London, 1925).

Hunter, W.W. : Bombay 1885 to 1890: A Study in Indian Administration (London, 1892).

Jackson, S. : The Sassoon's (London, 1968).

Jalbhoy, R.H. : The Portrait Gallery of Western India (Bombay, 1886).

Jeejeebhoy, J.R.B. : The Parsis in Bombay (Reprinted from Kaiser-E-Hind, Nowroze Number, 1940).

Jhabwala, S.H. : Sir Jamshedji Jeejeebhoy, Baronet (Bombay).

Jha, S.C. : Studies in the Development of Capitalism in India (Calcutta, 1963).

Joshi, P.B. : A Sketch of Early History of Bombay (1902).

Johnstone, Rev. J. : Abstract and Analysis of the Report of the Indian Education Commission (London, 1884).

Kaye, I.W. : The Administration of the East India Company—A History of India's Progress (London, 1853).

Knowles, L.C.A. : The Industrial and Commercial Revolutions in Great Britain during the Nineteenth Century (London, 1927).

Kulkarni, V.B. : History of the Indian Cotton Textile Industry (Bombay, 1979).

Lamb, H.B. : 'The Indian Business Communities and The Evolution of An Industrial Class' in Pacific Affairs, Vol . XXVIII, No. 2, June-1955.

Lenin, V.I. : Collected Works, Vol. IV (Moscow, 1963).

Leech E.R. : Elites in South Asia (Cambridge, Mukharjee S.N. (Ed.) 1971).

Maclean, James : A Guide to Bombay (Bombay, 1879).

Madgaonkar, G.N. : Mumbaiche Varnan (Marathi, 2nd ed.), (Bombay, 1961).

Malbari, B.M. : Bombay in the Making (London, 1910).

Malbari, B.M. : Gujarat and Gujarati's (Bombay, 1884).

Malcom, J. : Memoir of Central India including Malwa and adjoining provinces (London, 1832).

Manshardt. C. (ed.) : Bombay—Today and Tomorrow (Bombay, 1930).

Masani, R.P. : Dadabhoy Nauroji- The Grand Old Man of India (London, 1939).

Masselos, J.C. : Towards Nationalism, Public Institutions and Urban Politics in the 19th Century, (B'bay, 1974).

Marx, K. and Engles, F. : The Capital, 3 Vols. (Moscow, n.d.).

Max Weber : The Religion of India translated by Hans Gerth and Don Martindale.

Mazumdar, A.C. : Indian National Evolution (Madras, 1915).

Mehta, S.D. : The Indian Cotton Textile Industry: 1854-1954 (Bombay, 1955).

Milburn, William : Oriental Commerce of Principal Places in the East Indies, China and Japan, Vol. I (Black Party and Co. 1813).

Milton, 'Singer : When Great Tradition Modernise. An Anthropological Approach to Indian Civilization (New York, 1972).

Misra, B.B. : The Indian Middle Classes (London, 1961).

Morris, M.D. : The Emergence of an Industrial Lobour Force in India. A Study of Bombay Cotton Mill, 1854-1957 (Bombay, 1965).

Modi, Homi : Sir Phirozshah Mehta: A Political Biography (London, Reprinted in 1963).

Nehru, Jawaharlal : Discovery of India. (New Delhi, O.U.O. 1951).

Ovington, J. : A Voyage to Surat in the Year 1689, H.G. Rawlinson (ed.) (O.U.P. 1929).

Palekar, S.A. : Trade of India (Bombay, 1944).

Pandit, Nalini : Maharashtrateel Rashtravadacha Vikas: 1955-1972.

Pandit, D.P. : 'Creative Response in Indian Economy—A Regional Analysis' in Economic Weekly, Bombay, IX (February 23rd and March 2nd 1957).

Phatak, N.R. : Mumbai Nagari (Bombay, 1981).

Pavlov, V.I. : The Indian Capitalist Class (New Delhi, 1964).

Pavlov, V.I. : Historical Premises for India's Transition to Capitalism (Moscow, 1979).

Pillai, P.P. : Economic Conditions in India (London, 1925).

Pillai, P.P. : The Indian Cotton Mills Industry 1853-1922 in Indian Journal of Economics, Vol. V, Part 2 (October, 1924).

Postans, Mrs. Marianne : Western India in 1838 (Saunders & Otley, 1839).

Pearse, A.S : Cotton Industry of India (Manchester, 1930).

Prashad, Durga : Some Aspects of Indian Foreign Trade, 1757-1891 (London, 1932).

Pusalkar, A.D. & Dighe, V.G. : Bombay-Story of the Island City (Bombay, 1949).

Rajan, V.S. : An Economic History of India, 1757-1947 (Baroda, 1955).

Rao, C.H. : Indian Biographical Dictionary (Madras, 1950).

Rogers, A. : The Land Revenue of Bombay: A History of its Administrations, Rise and Progress (London, 1892).

Robert, Emma : Overland Journey to Bombay (London 1845).

Roy, M.N. : India in Transition (1917).

Rungta. R.S. : The Rise of Business Corporations in India-1851–1900 (Cambridge, 1970).

Rutnagur, S.M. : Bombay Industries: The Cotton Mills (Bombay, 1927).

Saklatwala, S.D. : History of the Mill owners Association (Bombay, n.d.).

Sarda Raju. A. : Economic Conditions in the Madras Presidency, 1800-1850 (Madras, 1941).

Sharma, T.R. : Location of Industries in India (Bombay, 1948).

Sharp, H : Selection from Educational Records, Part-I, 1920.

Shah, K.T. and Khambhata, K.J. : Wealth and Taxable Capacity of India (Bombay, 1924).

Sheppard, S.T. : Bombay (Bombay, 1932).

Sen. S. K. : Studies in Industrial Policy and Development of India, 1848-1926 (Calcutta, 1965).

Seal, A. : The Emergence of Indian Nationalism. Competition and Collaboration in the later Nineteenth Century (Cambridge, 1968).

Singh, Hiralal : Problems and Politics of the British in India 1885-1898 (Bombay, 1963).

Sleeman, W.H. : Rambles and Recollections of an Indian Officials, Vol. II (London, 1940).

Spear, Percival : India—A Modern Indian History (An Arbor, 1961).

Sulvan, R.J.F. : One Hundred Years of Bombay Chamber of Commerce 1836-1936, (Bombay, 1936).

Temple, Richard : Men and Events of my Time in India (London, 1882)

Timberg, Thomas : The Marwaris: From Traders to Industrialists (New Delhi, 1978).

Tindall, Gillion : City of Gold, The Biography of Bombay (London, 1882).

Thompson, E. & Garrat, G.T. : Rise and Fulfillment of British Rule in India (London, 1935).

Thorner, Daniel : Investment in Empire (Philadelphia, 1950).

Trevelyan, C.E. : On the Education of the People of India (London, 1838).

Turner, F.S. : British Opium Policy and its results in India and China (London, 1878).

Turkund, D.A. : Bombay Past and Present (Bombay, 1919).

Vakil, C. N. : Financial Development in Modern India (Bombay, 1925).

Vicziany, M. : 'Bombay Merchants and Structural Changes in the Export Community: 1850 to 1880', in K.N. Chaudhary and C. J. Dewey (ed.) Economy and Society: Essay in Indian Economic and Social History, (New Delhi, 1979).

Vedak, G. S. : A Life Sketch of the Hon. Mr. Jagannath Shankar Shet, (Bombay, 1937).

Wacha, D.E : A Financial Chapter in the History of Bombay (Bombay, 1910).

Wacha, D.E : Shells from the Sands of Bombay: My Recollections and Reminiscences, 1860-75 (Bombay, 1920).

Wacha, D.E : Premchand Roychand, His Early Life and Career (Bombay, 1913).

Wacha, R.F. : Mumbai no Bahar, Vol. I (Bombay, 1874).

Wadia, P.A. & Merchant K.T. : Our Economic Problem (2nd edition, Bombay, 1946).

Wadia, R.A. : Wadia Dockyard and Wadia Master Builders (Bombay, 1957).

Wadia, R.A. : A Financial Chapter in the History of Bombay City (Bombay, 1910).

Warden, F. : Report on the Landed Tenures of Bombay (Bombay, 1861).

Young, S.M. : East India Company's Arsenal (Oxford, 1937).

Index

L

Q

R

S